Unprofessional Essays

UNPROFESSIONAL ESSAYS

by

J. MIDDLETON MURRY

JONATHAN CAPE
THIRTY BEDFORD SQUARE · LONDON

FIRST PUBLISHED 1956

PRINTED IN GREAT BRITAIN BY
THE CAMELOT PRESS LTD., LONDON AND SOUTHAMPTON
BOUND BY A. W. BAIN & CO. LTD., LONDON

Prefatory Note

These essays – as the title of the book is intended to suggest – have been written wholly to please myself at a time
when I am no longer dependent on literary criticism for
my livelihood. Not that they are, necessarily, any the
better for that. But they are longer and more substantial
essays than I used to have the opportunity of writing
when I was a professional.

Thelnetham
April 23, 1955.

Contents

In Defence of Fielding

In Defence of Fielding

★

ON October 9, 1954, the two-hundredth anniversary of Henry Fielding's death evoked a singular article in *The Times Literary Supplement*. It dealt, in a series of curious judgments, with Fielding's novels in turn. First, *Joseph Andrews*:

> Setting out to make fun of Richardson's *Pamela* . . . to invert the sexes in the situation of the chaste servant pestered by the lascivious employer, he found that his characters, particularly the delightful Parson Adams, were becoming rounded and real and that they needed a wider range of activity than that offered by the working out of a not particularly novel smutty joke.

Most of that is critical commonplace; only the final phrase is original, and stupid. The situation of the attempted seduction of a reluctant young man by an amorous woman is not indeed novel, but surely it is not a smutty joke.

After passing lightly and condescendingly over *Amelia*, venturing no opinion of his own upon it, the critic discusses *Jonathan Wild*.

> George Saintsbury, one of Fielding's heartiest admirers, classed it with Thackeray's *Barry Lyndon* as one of

the few English masterpieces of irony, outside Swift.

Probably no modern critic would share Saintsbury's high estimate of these two books. A consideration of why not, and why modern critics see neither Fielding nor Thackeray – the novelist who owes most to Fielding – as bulking so large in 'the great tradition' as Saintsbury saw them, throws some light on shifts of taste over the past fifty years. The modern critic likes irony – 'irony', indeed, like 'ambiguity', 'ambivalence', 'paradox', 'complexity', is one of the words he persistently overworks – but he likes it more than one layer deep. *Jonathan Wild the Great* and *Barry Lyndon* are two works constructed on the same principle. In one, the life of a criminal is recounted in the tone of a biography of a great man; in the other a mean rascal tells his own story without apparently seeing what a mean rascal he is. The assumption in both cases is that neither the author of the story nor his readers could possibly be involved in such doings as are held up for reprobation. It is a smug assumption, and the smugness – the presumption of virtuous superiority – infects the tone of both books.

The last two sentences, as applied to *Jonathan Wild* – with *Barry Lyndon* we are not concerned – are astonishing. It is difficult to attach any meaning at all to the statement that Fielding's 'assumption' is that neither he nor his readers could behave like Jonathan Wild. Wild is represented by Fielding as what he seems to have been in reality – a clever, cruel, mean and ruthless knave. Fielding does not 'assume' that he could not behave like Wild; he knows it. To speak of his obvious contempt for Wild, and for those who glamourized him, as 'a smug assumption of virtuous superiority which infects the tone' of the book strikes me as sheer nonsense – if not worse, an example of the debasement of moral standards by the current literary cant of conditioning and compassion. For it is hard to imagine what the critic could have had in mind, unless perhaps the possibility that in 1954 a very different writer from Fielding – and one quite inconceivable in 1742 – might present the facts of a career like Wild's in a way that would arouse some sympathy for him. But to use this bare possibility (if indeed it is one) as a basis for depreciating Fielding's novel is a perversity.

Still more perverse is the writer's judgment of *Tom Jones:*

Tom Jones, in fact must rank as Fielding's greatest achievement largely because of the beautiful turn of the plot which forces Fielding to transcend, for once, the genial tolerance of the man-about-town. Tom Jones, a foundling, who does not know who his parents are, has a brief affair at a country inn with an attractive woman in early middle age, Mrs. Waters. Fielding, by the tone of burlesque heroics in which he presents the episode, seems to be making light of it, and even conniving at it. Yet it is the first step in a moral progress downhill; Tom, when he reaches London, becomes – though he is genuinely and passionately in love with a sweet and innocent girl – the kept playboy of an elderly and not very attractive woman of quality. And then, much later in the book, evidence comes to light which suggests, with terrible plausibility, both to Tom and the reader, that Mrs. Waters is the mother whom Tom has never met. Fielding's connivance was a pretence. He has sprung a trap on Tom and us; he has made us realize – as a serious novelist always makes us realize; and as a frivolous novelist often tries to make us forget – that actions have their consequences. The past is not in *Tom Jones*, as in a genuinely picaresque novel, a place we move away from; it is something which exerts a continuing and possibly fatal pressure on the present. It is this sense of the moral structure of life which makes Fielding important.

It must be a curiously constituted mind which can receive that particular impression from *Tom Jones*. It could be derived, one thinks, only from a wilful distortion of the book: the virtue of which, in this strange perspective, is that, at one moment in the history of the episode with Mrs. Waters, Fielding 'transcends, *for once*, the genial tolerance of the man-about-town'. What to a more normal sensibility constitutes the one doubtful moment in the book – the one moment at which we feel that Fielding *may* have sounded a false note, by suggesting an awful possibility outside the range of the experience he invites us to partake – becomes in this vision the one thing which makes the book considerable: 'the only novel of its period which rises at its crisis, to a pitch of tragic horror'. It would be safe to say that no one else has felt like that about Tom Jones. Or, at least, one hopes it would be safe. For there is no knowing where we may have got to.

At any rate it is, if not safe, at least imperative to say that this judgment is positively perverse. It is buttressed by obvious misrepresentations. For example, to say that Tom's affair with Mrs. Waters is 'the first step in a moral progress downhill' is to defy not only the constant impression made by the novel, but the facts it records. What of Tom's affair with Molly Seagrim? Does that count for nothing? If not, why not? Why does not his 'moral progress downhill' begin there? But, more important, this moral deterioration of Tom is an invention of the critic's. After his affair with Mrs. Waters, Tom behaves, on his arrival in London, with the utmost humanity and generosity to the wretched 'highwayman' Anderson, who turns out to be his landlady's destitute friend. And to represent the affair with Lady Bellaston as a descent into the depths of moral turpitude is to do violence to Fielding's plain intention, and to distort Tom's character. There is no excuse for this distortion. Tom's character is lavishly and convincingly presented by his creator. His sexual offences – if offences they are – are intimately connected with his generosity of soul.

Worst of all, to argue that, because for a moment Tom mistakenly believes that his affair with Mrs. Waters has landed him in the appalling position of Oedipus, Fielding has 'a sense of the moral structure of life', which 'makes him important'; while at the same time declaring that this moment is quite isolated and unparalleled: that in it '*for once* Fielding transcends the genial tolerance of the man-about-town', is to assert that Fielding is important only by accident – by virtue of something quite exceptional and adventitious in his work – and to discover in the novel the representation of 'a moral structure in life' which does not exist, while completely ignoring the one which does. The phrase, 'the genial tolerance of the man-about-town' gives the critic away even more than his previous phrases about 'the smutty joke' of *Joseph Andrews*, or the 'virtuous superiority' in the author of *Jonathan Wild*. They are the phrases of a writer who does not like Fielding and who, one suspects, would never have read him, except for the purpose of writing an article about him.

By an odd contrast, *The Times* itself of the same anniversary day carried another brief article on Fielding, containing this judgment:

> The lessons to be learnt from Fielding are still not ex-
> hausted. There is not, for instance in all English fiction, a
> hero as natural and endearing as Tom Jones. And how is
> his virtue conveyed? Simply by setting down on paper
> without any complication and in the simplest manner the
> faithful image of a lively young man, full of faults and
> contradictory aspirations. It does not sound a very difficult
> art. Yet the learned novelists of the present day, nurtured
> on Freud and borne up on the surface of life by water-
> wings existential and positivist, do only half as well.

Who would believe these two critics were writing of the same book? The criticism of the second one may not be very profound, but it registers the all-important fact: that Tom Jones himself is a nonpareil for charm and natural manliness among the heroes of English fiction. Who would suspect that from the perverse and alembicated refinements of the first critic?

§

There are signs in his essay that his perversity proceeds from an effort to be original at all costs. He apparently has one eye on Dr. Leavis – the reference to *The Great Tradition* points in that direction – and the other eye on Saintsbury: no eye at all being left for the object, which is Henry Fielding and his novels. I have no quarrel at all with his looking

for a middle line between Saintsbury's extravagant enthusiasm and Dr. Leavis's chilly depreciation; but the middle
line must be drawn through Fielding's own works, not
through a pretentious simulacrum of them. Dr. Leavis's own
attitude, wrong-headed though I believe it to be – is much to
be preferred to the bogus profundity of the critic of *The
Times Literary Supplement*. Dr. Leavis is nothing if not forth-
right.

> Fielding (he says) deserves the place of importance given
> to him in literary histories, but he hasn't the kind of
> classical distinction we are also invited to credit him with.
> He is important not because he leads to Mr. J. B. Priestley
> but because he leads to Jane Austen, to appreciate whose
> distinction is to feel that life is not long enough to permit
> of one's giving much time to Fielding or any to Mr.
> Priestley.

There is a piece of bad manners there, in the gratuitous
reference to Mr. Priestley, which may have raised a laugh in
the Cambridge lecture room, but looks embarrassing in
print. But that is beside the point. It is plain that Dr. Leavis
does not enjoy Fielding. That, I think, is his misfortune. But
his reasons for not enjoying Fielding are interesting.

> That the eighteenth century, which hadn't much lively
> reading to choose from, but had much leisure, should have
> found *Tom Jones* exhilarating, is not surprising; nor is it
> that Scott, and Coleridge, should have been able to give
> that work superlative praise. Standards are formed in com-
> parison, and what opportunities had they for that. But
> the conventional talk about the 'perfect construction' of

Tom Jones . . . is absurd. There can't be subtlety of organization without richer matter to organize, and subtler
interests than Fielding has to offer. He is credited with
range and variety and it is true that some episodes take
place in the country and some in Town, some in the
churchyard and some in the inn, some on the high-road
and some in the bedchamber and so on. But we haven't
to read a very large proportion of *Tom Jones* in order to
discover the limits of the essential interests it has to offer
us. Fielding's attitudes, and his concern with human
nature, are simple, and not such as to produce an effect of
anything but monotony (on a mind, that is, demanding
more than external action) when exhibited at the length of
an 'epic in prose'. What he *can* do appears to best effect
in *Joseph Andrews*. *Jonathan Wild*, with its famous irony,
seems to me mere hobblehoydom (much as one applauds
the determination to explode the gangster hero) and by
Amelia Fielding has gone soft.

In so far as Dr. Leavis is tilting against the conventional and
stereotyped estimates of Fielding, such as appear and reappear
in the text-books of English literature, he has my sympathy.
I agree that the praise of the superlative construction of *Tom
Jones* is overdone, though to be sure it does not refer to what
Dr. Leavis means by 'subtlety of organization' at all, but only
to the contrivance of the plot, which is excellent, but within
the reach of something less than genius. I agree, too, that the
conventional – or is it merely Saintsburian? – laudation of
Jonathan Wild as the masterpiece of sustained irony in fiction
is extravagant. The irony is neither subtle nor sustained. And
a good deal more may be urged against Fielding that Dr.

In Defence of Fielding

Leavis does not urge at all: the prefaces in *Tom Jones*, though by no means uninteresting, are a nuisance, and the digressive tales a clumsiness. But, when all that can be objected has been objected, the simple fact remains that *Joseph Andrews*, and *Tom Jones*, and *Amelia* are absorbing stories, and *Jonathan Wild* (though it ranks far behind any of these) is a good and at times a very amusing one.

Because Dr. Leavis has savoured the very different satisfactions that Jane Austen, George Eliot, Henry James, and Joseph Conrad have to offer, has he become incapable of taking delight in Fielding's novels? If so, it is a lamentable end to a lifetime meritoriously spent in literary scrutiny; and still more lamentable, when this acquired incapacity, which looks like an occupational disease, leads him to declare, in effect, that no one who truly appreciates his four 'great English novelists' can possibly also appreciate Fielding. The essential quality of a great novelist, according to Dr. Leavis, 'being an intense moral preoccupation' with the problems which life puts to a mature mind, and since, according to him, Fielding has no such moral preoccupation, it follows that Fielding can have only a historical interest for such a mind.

I am a little surprised that Dr. Leavis, who so greatly and justly admires Jane Austen and George Eliot, and who points out with evident satisfaction that 'it is not for nothing that George Eliot admired Jane Austen's work profoundly', should not have noticed that George Eliot also profoundly admired the work of Fielding. Had he done so, it might have caused him to hesitate before declaring quite so peremptorily that 'to appreciate the distinction of Jane Austen is to feel that life isn't long enough to permit of one's giving much time to Fielding'. George Eliot felt that life was long enough to do both, although one would imagine, from her achievement, that she had no more time to spare than Dr. Leavis has. Probably, Dr. Leavis considers that her spending time on Fielding was a lamentable aberration, best passed over in silence.

I do not doubt that Dr. Leavis is sincere in his depreciation of Fielding. Fielding obviously bores him: and it is honest of him to say so. If he had left it at that, perhaps there would have been no more to be said. But he does not leave it at that. He very distinctly implies that it is reasonable and right for him to be bored by Fielding, because he is a person with a mature mind, and the intense moral interest that goes with it: and a mature mind must of necessity be bored by Fielding. That is too deliberately provocative to be passed over. I like to think – however presumptuously – that my mind is only a little less mature than Dr. Leavis's, and that my moral pre-occupation is not wholly inferior to his own. Yet I admire and enjoy Fielding. So I am compelled, in self-defence, to excogitate some plausible reason why Dr. Leavis's maturity of mind is bored by Fielding, while mine is not. I humbly suggest it is because Fielding's novels do not lend themselves to the kind of treatment which Dr. Leavis delights to exercise upon the novel. They bring devilishly little grist to his particular mill. They are evasive and recalcitrant to his highly specialized mental processes. The moral preoccupations with which they are concerned – and really, in spite of Dr. Leavis's pronunciamento, they have each a moral preoccupation – are not of the sort that makes an impression upon him. Their durable achievement, in the creation of characters of whose reality we are convinced and who abide in the memory, is one which he cannot recognize because he cannot account for it by his critical methods. Not that I pretend to be able to account for it by mine. But at least I recognize the fact with admiration and gratitude, and hold that to dismiss this achievement as insignificant – or at any rate as giving no claim whatever to the title of 'a great novelist' – is not to clarify but to confuse criticism.

I have enjoyed, and been stimulated by, Dr. Leavis's positive appreciations in *The Great Tradition*. But, unfortunately, it seems to be inherent in Dr. Leavis's mental constitution, that he cannot really appreciate something unless he is depreciating something else. For example, he uncovers hidden excellences in Dickens's *Hard Times*; but he cannot do this, without at the same time declaring that 'of all Dickens's works it is the one which has all the strength of his genius, together with a strength no other of them can show – that of a completely serious work of art'. That means that *Hard Times* is Dickens's masterpiece: which it certainly is not. And the plain truth is that *Hard Times* has *not* all the strength of Dickens's genius. I can only conclude that there are important facets of Dickens's genius to which Dr. Leavis is wholly irresponsive. And I suspect that those facets of his genius are precisely those which are totally unamenable to treatment by Dr. Leavis's critical apparatus. Therefore, they ought not exist. From that it is only a step to declaring that they do not exist.

Dr. Leavis is an influential critic. I have a vivid memory of a review in *The Times Literary Supplement* which began with the impressive words: 'Jonathan Swift, as Dr. Leavis says, is a great English writer.' I felt relieved. Swift was safe, after all. But, I fear, Fielding is not. And though I realize that nothing I can say can avert the dread sentence, in some future issue of *The Times Literary Supplement*, that 'Fielding, as Dr. Leavis says, is an unimportant novelist', I am constrained, by piety, affection and gratitude, to venture a few naïve words on his behalf.

§

I had better put my cards on the table. I admire Fielding the writer; and I admire Fielding the man. *Tom Thumb* never ceases to delight me; *Jonathan Wild*, though I am far from thinking it the masterpiece of sustained irony it has been claimed, seems to me a still vital book, with some superb comic-ironic episodes; *Joseph Andrews*, quite apart from its own intrinsic quality – unequal but oh, how alive! – has the fascination of being a genuine transition piece; I reckon both *Tom Jones* and *Amelia* as great novels, by any standard – absorbing stories of the vicissitudes of permanently credible human beings. I am unable to prefer one to the other: that one seems to be the better which I happen to be reading. I admire Fielding's labours as the Bow Street magistrate. Finally, I admire the man who wrote *The Voyage to Lisbon*. That is a heroic book. Its very obscurities (and there are not a few), its often hurried and slip-shod writing, its sometimes convoluted thought, all the plain and painful evidences that it was written under pressure without time or energy for revision – are so many reminders that the mere writing of it was a heroism, undertaken partly as an anodyne to the physical agonies Fielding endured on that mercilessly protracted voyage from the combination of asthma, dropsy and gout which racked his emaciated body. Yet, were it not for the casual mention of surgeons tapping his swollen stomach, or of his inability to move himself, one would never suppose it was the journal of a tortured and dying man. He is far more concerned for his wife's sufferings from the ache of a rotten tooth than for his own. These we have to imagine.

It is not a masterpiece of literature; but it is the work of a noble nature. The marvel is that it was written at all. What, one wonders, would or could Keats have written on his like voyage? The imagination flinches at the thought. But, almost involuntarily, we compare the last voyages of these two great souls. For sheer physical discomfort (if so mild a word is applicable) Fielding's was the more appalling. It took him forty-two days to get from London to Lisbon, whereas Keats reached Naples in thirty-four. Fielding arrived at Lisbon on August 7 and died on October 8. He lasted exactly two months, Keats lasted four. He reached Naples on October 21 and died on February 23. But the mental torments of the two are not commensurable. Fielding had his wife with him; Keats was being borne irrevocably away from his beloved. Fielding had the solace of having done his life's work; Keats the fearful, though mistaken, conviction that his had hardly been begun.

And, of course, Keats belongs to us in a way Fielding never can. How many of Fielding's letters do we possess? Perhaps a half-dozen, and not one of them intimately personal. When the Gordon rioters burned down his brother John's house in 1780, there perished almost certainly in the conflagration a mass of Fielding's correspondence and manuscripts. The accident was malign, but not unpatterned, for Fielding had finally worn himself out in the struggle against the civic anarchy which made possible the Gordon riots. It is as though the gradually expiring lawlessness of London had made one final effort to annihilate him. What would we not give for one such letter from Fielding as Keats wrote to his brother and sister in America?

That is a very idle dream: for few things could be more certain than that Fielding never wrote any such letters. There is, at the best, a rather grim impersonality about the early eighteenth century. At a given point, the curtain invariably descends – not wholly unlike that which now conceals from us what is happening in the minds and souls who live in the vast totalitarian empire dominated by Moscow. There was in England of the early eighteenth century, a life-style to which everybody who was anybody seems to have conformed instinctively, without perceptible self-mutilation. It was inimical to the expression of the particular and the idiosyncratic. And Fielding himself though he was evidently in rebellion against it could not greatly escape the pattern.

Towards the end of his life Fielding returned in *The Covent Garden Journal* to a favourite inquiry of his – the nature of humour, and maintained that truly humorous characters could only be found where there is complete exemption from 'those rules of behaviour which are expressed in the general term of good-breeding', which consists in 'the art of conducting yourself by certain common and general rules, by which means, if they were universally observed, the whole world would appear (as all courtiers actually do) to be, in their external behaviour at least, but one and the same person'. Good breeding is, therefore, 'the very bane of the ridiculous, that is to say, of all humourous characters.' Fielding was obviously in two minds. With half of himself he is on the side of 'good breeding' – that is, when he understands it, as he had expounded it in a previous essay, as obedience to the rule of doing to others as you would they should do to you; with the other half he regards it as a code of behaviour purely external, repressive of individuality and spontaneity. His own

supreme comic character, Parson Adams, was a perfect
example of good breeding in the former sense, but a rebel
against it in the latter.

§

Indeed, the chief indictment brought against Fielding's
novels by contemporary criticism was that they were 'low'.
In *Joseph Andrews* he came near to representing, what one of
his fictitious correspondents in *The Covent Garden Journal*
stated as a fact, 'that all the wit and humour of this kingdom
was to be found in the ale houses'. And not the wit and humour
only, but the charity, the generosity, and the honest emotion.
Certainly, he did believe, and showed, that the good nature –
the natural sympathy and benevolence – which he prized
above all other human qualities, was as frequent in low society
as in high: more frequent, indeed, according to the testimony
of his first novel. Who are Joseph Andrews's real benefactors
on his eventful journey homewards? The postillion, who lent
him his greatcoat, and was subsequently transported for
robbing a hen-roost; Betty the chambermaid, who got him
the tea he longed for in spite of Mrs. Tow-wouse, but was in
some other respects no better than she should be; and the
pedlar who lent Parson Adams his all, amounting to six shil-
lings and sixpence? The only one who belongs to a higher
walk of society is Mr. Wilson, and he is a man who has
deliberately retired from it in disgust of its deceptions as well
as of his own follies. No doubt, in *Joseph Andrews* Fielding was
giving our betters the worst of it, in reaction against the rather
fulsome picture of the upper-classes drawn in Richardson's
Pamela. In his novels taken as a whole he holds the balance
pretty level between the classes. Generosity of soul, he seems

to say, is rare in either; but where it exists, it reveals class-distinction as the accident he asserted it to be.

This was the attitude, one feels, which chiefly earned for Fielding the derogatory epithet of 'low', and in particular his insistence that the particular manifestation of generosity of soul, which he believed was essential to the experience of love, was entirely independent of social position. He seems to have come to a full awareness of his own instinctive attitude through the impact upon him of Richardson's *Pamela*. That brilliant, but unsatisfactory book, shocked him profoundly. No doubt he was as impressed as we are by Richardson's narrative skill, and the subtlety with which he delineates the growth of Pamela's passion for her designing and unscrupulous master; but he drew the line absolutely at accepting it for what Richardson claimed it to be, a sound and edifying moral tale. As an example of 'virtue rewarded' it stuck in his throat. 'Virginity exorts its price', would, in Fielding's opinion, have been a much more accurate sub-title. Pamela's 'virtue' was a spurious article. Fielding let himself go about it, merrily and coarsely, in *Shamela* (which is almost certainly his, though he never owned it); but he was not satisfied with that immediate explosion. *Pamela*, whose influence was enormous, was not to be combated effectively in that way.

So he set to again, and this time, in *Joseph Andrews* all his faculties were engaged. It is evident from the book that Fielding began with no particular plan beyond the brilliant and immediate one of giving Pamela a footman brother, who was a prodigy of 'virtue' like herself, and representing him as assailed by his aristocratic mistress, whose bodily attractions were equal to her appetite. The opening scenes between Lady Booby and Joseph are magnificent: for verve and comic brilliance they are not surpassed, if indeed they are equalled, by anything that follows in the book. But, obviously, if the story was to be developed from that basis – as a sustained and deadly parody of *Pamela* – it would have had to proceed by a fairly patient exposition of Joseph's skill in leading Lady Booby on until her passion got the better of her pride and she agreed to marry him. Not only would this have made Joseph a character thoroughly uncongenial to Fielding, but, because nature would insist on breaking in, Joseph's character had already, in the Lady Booby scenes, been so presented that such a development was impossible. Her ladyship's person had been made very attractive; and the invitation of her naked bed irresistible to a young man of normal composition. And Fielding, on the whole, agreed with Shakespeare:

> And, when a woman woos, what woman's son
> Will sourly leave her till she have prevailed?

Joseph, in refusing the temptation, would plainly have been revealed as a prig, in Fielding's estimation, had he not been able to set up what Fielding regarded as the one absolutely valid defence against the charge of inflicting upon a comely woman the humiliation of rejecting her offered beauty: namely, the fact that he was already in love.

Not that Fielding would have been very severe on Joseph even if he had succumbed to Lady Booby: he certainly would not have rejected him as a monster, or concluded that it was impossible for him to be genuinely in love with his Fanny. It was obviously for him an interesting and important problem in sexual ethics, for he treated it copiously in both *Tom Jones* and *Amelia*, where the heroes have not the advantage – a real one in Fielding's eyes – of having been educated by Parson

Adams. Tom Jones falls three times. His initial amour with Molly Seagrim, which at first made him relatively insensible to the charms of Sophia, does not count; but his resumption of it, at the very moment when, slightly drunk, he had taken out his knife to carve Sophia's name upon a tree, certainly does. His affair with Mrs. Waters at the Upton inn also counts; and so, more seriously still, does his intrigue with Lady Bellaston. Common to them all is that the women make the running. And there is to be said for Tom Jones throughout, that he is never really certain, until the very end of the book, that his love for Sophia is not utterly hopeless. The chief difference between his various amours is that, whereas with Molly Seagrim and Mrs. Waters Tom falls to their physical allure – Mrs. Waters' lovely bosom attracts his eyes at their first encounter – it is otherwise with Lady Bellaston. The process of his and her entanglement is admirably described. Her ladyship is prepared to fall for him by the rapturous account of her maid; the growth of her passion – for passion it becomes – is hastened when she sees him, by Mrs. Fitzpatrick's contrivance; the flame is fanned by his confession to her at the masquerade of his entire devotion to Sophia. Then Tom is in the toils.

> Jones had never less inclination to an amour than at present; but gallantry to the ladies was among his principles of honour; and he held it as much incumbent upon him to accept a challenge to love, as if it had been a challenge to fight.

Lady Bellaston's generosity to him rivets the chain. And though Fielding carries his realism to the point of hinting very plainly that her ladyship's breath, like her character, was no better than it should be, he is obviously not at all unsympathetic to Tom's notion of what his honour required. After enlarging on the fadedness of her ladyship's charms, he says:

> Though Jones saw all these discouragements on the one side, he felt his obligations full as strongly on the other; nor did he less plainly discern the ardent passion from whence those obligations proceeded, the extreme violence of which if he failed to equal, he well knew the lady would think him ungrateful; and what is worse, he would have thought himself so. He knew the tacit consideration upon which all her favours were conferred; and as his necessity obliged him to accept them, so his honour, he concluded, forced him to pay the price. This therefore he resolved to do, whatever misery it cost him, from that great principle of justice, by which the laws of some countries oblige a debtor, who is no otherwise capable of discharging his debt, to become the slave of his creditor.

Naturally, Fielding leaves a good deal to our imagination in this delicate matter: but he means to compel us to imagine. And it is fairly plain that, however irksome it might be for a truly good-natured man 'to support love with gratitude', Fielding means us to believe that Tom did. His lack of such positive physical desire for Lady Bellaston as had taken him into the arms of Molly and Mrs. Waters was supplied by his genuine gratitude to her. The defect of the one passion was filled by the fullness of the other. And we are sufficiently convinced of this to feel that the potential sordidness of the relation is dispelled.

§

It seems that in this affair between Tom Jones and Lady Bellaston, Fielding was deliberately exploring the human reality of the situation which he had adumbrated, as a mere abstract and satirical possibility, in *Joseph Andrews*. Originally it entered his mind simply as the comic converse of the relation between Pamela and her concupiscent master, Mr. B——. That, as it stood, he could not develop with veracity. His plan compelled him to depict Joseph as resisting the very positive charms and seductions of Lady Booby; but, though he had fortified him with a moral education from Parson Adams and a genuine devotion to Fanny, Fielding, it is pretty plain, did not really believe in Joseph's behaviour. It was, in the simple sense, too good to be true, when judged by his criterion of the natural behaviour of a good-natured young man. On the other hand, it was equally impossible to sustain the satire on *Pamela*, by representing Joseph as cunningly trading his virtue for a marriage with her ladyship. So Fielding virtually dropped the situation altogether: he brought Abraham Adams on to the centre of the stage, and deposed Joseph to a merely secondary role, in which the fact of his being rather a lay-figure could do no great harm.

In other words, *Tom Jones* consists largely in a realization of possibilities which Fielding had suggested to himself in the course of writing *Joseph Andrews*. Tom is Joseph, as Sophia is Fanny, made real flesh and blood. Such a transmutation was not necessary in the case of Lady Booby, for she was already real – much the most real character in the book, if we except Adams, who belongs to a different order of creation. Lady Bellaston had only to be made different; and perhaps that is the original reason why she is definitely older than the still youthful Lady Booby. But Fielding's invention served him well, for it enabled him to represent his hero as betrayed not again by physical appetite but by his own notions of what gallantry and gratitude and honour required.

It is often forgotten by those who cannot help thinking Tom Jones slightly disreputable that he never lays siege to a woman; it is always the women who beleaguer him. Tom's trouble is that he cannot find it in his heart to repulse them: and this is because he is, fundamentally, an idealist about women. Rightly or wrongly, he discerns generosity in the woman's offer of herself to him, to which if he does not respond, he is self-condemned as ungenerous. This does not fit at all with conventional notions of the virtue of chastity, male or female; but it is not incongruous with a delicate and sensitive humanity. Much of Tom's potent charm for us consists in the real, as distinct from and even directly opposed to the conventional, purity he possesses. He is a really innocent soul, where Joseph Andrews is only abstractly innocent; and though he loses some of his boyish naïvety, he never loses his innocence. With Molly, he is naïve; he entirely fails to see that she is inveigling him. It is not vanity which persuades him he is the responsible party, but his incapacity to conceive that a young woman should be determined to seduce him. And when he has possessed her his reaction is that of a naturally generous soul to generosity. He was, Fielding says, one of those who 'can never receive any kind of satisfaction from another, without loving the creature to whom that satisfaction is owing, and without making its well-being in some sort necessary to their own ease'.

When he meets Mrs. Waters, he is evidently more

experienced: he does not delude himself with the notion that he is the aggressor. He is aware that the lady is offering herself to him; and she knows well that the sight of her bosom has lighted a small flame in him.

> She seemed to be at the least of the middle age, nor had her face much appearance of beauty; but her clothes being torn from all the upper part of her body, her breasts, which were well formed and extremely white, attracted the eyes of her deliverer, and for a few moments they stood silent, and gazing on one another.

She does not hesitate to fan the flame by the same means. She deliberately refused Tom's offer of his overcoat, when he walked before her to the Upton inn, and seized every opportunity she could to make him look back at her. Presumably, though Fielding did not record it, she consented to let her devastating bosom be covered, when they reached the village. Finally, she completes her conquest of him by 'carelessly letting the handkerchief drop from her neck' and 'unmasking the royal battery'. Tom really had not much chance.

Nor was Mrs. Waters at all deeply perturbed when she discovered that Tom's heart was already engaged.

> The beauty of Jones highly charmed her eye; but as she could not see his heart, she gave herself no concern about it. She could feast heartily at the table of love, without reflecting that some other already had been, or hereafter might be, feasted with the same repast. A sentiment which, if it deals but little in refinement, deals, however, much in substance; and is less capricious, and perhaps less ill-natured and selfish, than the desires of those females who

can be contented enough to abstain from the possession of their lovers, provided they are sufficiently satisfied that no one else possesses them.

Fielding's own sentiment about such women as Mrs. Waters is evident. They are more good-natured and more generous than many nominally more virtuous. He quite likes Mrs. Waters, and so do we. She is completely unmercenary, and she retained sufficient affection for Tom to do him a great service; and we may be pretty sure she made her lover happy, for all that Tom 'detested the very thoughts of her' when he learned that Sophia had been at the inn and wanting to see him while he was otherwise engaged.

§

Behind all this behaviour of Tom's is not 'the genial tolerance of a man about town' in his creator, but a positive moral conviction, in the important sphere of the ethics of the sexual relation. Tom, his creator believes and convinces us, is fundamentally good: and as much as his appetite it is his goodness that leads him into his entanglements. In a different sphere, he manifests the same delicacy when he refuses to be the instrument for conveying Allworthy's sentence of banishment to Blifil. 'What might perhaps be justice from another tongue would from mine be insult.' Allworthy is a good man, indeed, but he has not Tom's imaginative sympathy, though he comes to recognize and admire it in Tom. 'Oh, my child, to what goodness have I been so long blind!' This moral discrimination in the portrayal of Tom is as sound as it is subtle, but it is seldom explicitly distinguished even by admirers of Fielding: partly perhaps because they are content to accept the naturalness of Tom's character while they are engrossed by his adventures, and partly because Fielding himself seems to play it down by representing it as 'good-nature', which has come to mean something different and much more vague than Fielding intended by it. In his essay *On the Knowledge of the Characters of Men*, he drew a distinction which is of cardinal importance to an understanding of *Tom Jones* and its hero. He speaks of 'the gross but common mistake of good-humour for good-nature' –

> Two qualities, so far from bearing any resemblance to each other that they are almost opposites. Good-nature is that benevolent and amiable temper of mind which disposes us to feel the misfortunes and enjoy the happiness of others; and consequently pushes us on to promote the latter and prevent the former; and that without any abstract contemplation of the beauty of virtue, and without the allurements or terrors of religion. Now, good-humour is nothing more than the triumph of the mind, when reflecting on its own happiness, and that perhaps from having compared it with the inferior happiness of others.

In short, good nature is a natural and effortless goodness expressing itself as imaginative sympathy with the joys and sorrows of others: as distinct from the goodness which is constrained either by religious fears, or by the pursuit of a rationally conceived idea of virtue: both of which Fielding holds up to ridicule in Thwackum and Square. He means that both these kinds of goodness tend to hypocrisy (perfected in their pupil Blifil), which is intolerable to him; and, even at their best, he believes them to be essentially inferior to the goodness which is natural and spontaneous, and finds expression in sympathy.

Fielding holds that good nature, in this sense, alone is capable of love. In the prefatory chapter to Book VI of *Tom Jones*, as against the philosophers who declare that there is no such thing as love, but only appetite, he defines love in precisely the same terms as he defines good nature.

I desire of the philosophers to grant there is in some human breasts a kind and benevolent disposition which is gratified by contributing to the happiness of others. That in this gratification alone, as in friendship, in parental and filial affection, there is a great and exquisite delight. That if we will not call such a disposition love, we have no name for it. That though the pleasures arising from such pure love may be heightened and sweetened by the assistance of amorous desires, yet the former may subsist alone, nor are they destroyed by the intervention of the latter.

Love between man and woman is a particular manifestation of this general disposition.

This love when it operates towards one of a different sex is very apt, towards its complete gratification, to call in the aid of that hunger which I have mentioned above [sexual appetite]; and which it is so far from abating that it heightens all its delights to a degree scarce imaginable by those who have never been susceptible of any other emotions than what have proceeded from appetite alone.

This consummation of physical passion between a man and a woman of good nature who love one another, Fielding holds, very definitely, to be the supreme felicity attainable on earth. And that is the end of Tom's adventurous pilgrimage. When Sophia and he are in bed together, Fielding declares, quite simply and sincerely:

> Thus, reader, we have at length brought our history to a conclusion, in which, to our great pleasure, though contrary perhaps to thy expectation, Mr. Jones appears to be the happiest of all humankind: for what happiness this world affords equal to the possession of such a woman as Sophia, I sincerely own I have never yet discovered.

It is Fielding's genuine conviction that this is the *summum bonum* for mortals: and Tom shares it. But until the very end of the novel he believes this felicity unattainable by him. He is in love with Sophia and believes she may be with him; but she is determined that she will not marry him without her father's consent, which it is hopeless to expect: and Tom, in disgrace with fortune and men's eyes, accepts it as right and proper that she should not. Doubtless, were he a Galahad, he would refuse all substitutes; but he is not. As Fielding puts it, when Tom falls to Molly the second time, after having caught her with Square, and in the very height and ecstasy of his dream of Sophia, 'Jones probably thought one woman better than none' – a sentiment which, if not very exalted, is natural. And Tom, as we have seen, is always grateful to his partners: to Molly and Mrs. Waters for their physical kindness, and to Lady Bellaston for another sort of generosity: while, for their part, the ladies are not a whit behind in gratitude. Mrs. Waters afterwards thinks wistfully of him 'to whom I owed such perfect happiness'. So that Tom is, very definitely, not one of those 'who have never been susceptible of any other emotions than what have proceeded from appetite alone'. He is, if anything, rather a backward lover; it is being desired that makes him desire. And it is characteristic of him that, out of a kind of chivalry, he is unjust to himself when, at the end he reproaches himself to Sophia.

'After what is past, sir, can you expect that I should take you upon your word?'

He replied, 'Don't believe me upon my word; I have a better security, a pledge for my constancy, which it is impossible to see and to doubt.' 'What is that?' said Sophia, a little surprised. 'I will show you, my charming angel', cried Jones, seizing her hand and carrying her to the glass . . .

Sophia blushed and half smiled; but, forcing again her brow into a frown,

'If I am to judge', said she, 'of the future by the past, my image will no more remain in your heart when I am out of your sight, than it will in this glass when I am out of the room.' 'By heaven, by all that is sacred!' said Jones, 'it never was out of my heart. The delicacy of your sex cannot conceive the grossness of ours, nor how little one sort of amour has to do with the heart.'

That was unfair to himself. If grossness there was, which is disputable, the sexes had fairly shared it in Tom's affairs. But it was Tom's habit always to take the blame upon himself in everything, and above all where women were concerned. If he had tried to tell the real truth, as Fielding knew it, to Sophia, it would have been interesting. But she, of course, had to reply to what he actually said.

'I will never marry a man', replied Sophia, very gravely, 'who shall not learn refinement enough to be as incapable as I am of making the distinction.'

It sounds good; it is good. Yet we wonder what precisely *is* the distinction. But Tom understands.

> 'I will learn it', said Jones. 'I have learnt it already. The first moment of hope that Sophia might be my wife taught it me at once; and all the rest of her sex from that moment became as little the objects of desire to my sense as of passion to my heart.'

In short, as soon as Tom knew that his felicity with his beloved was attainable, desire and love became identical: no distinction was possible any more. But so long as this fruition seemed unattainable, desire was kindled for any attractive woman who would be kind. Perhaps it is a difficult sexual ethic to formulate: but, within Fielding's fundamental concept of good nature, conceived as fairly embracing the sexual with all the rest of human relations, it is entirely convincing. In *Tom Jones* Fielding exhibits it in a person and in act, and carries his point triumphantly. Good nature is better than goodness. 'There is not in all English fiction, a hero as natural and endearing as Tom Jones' – and few heroines, one must add, more spirited, more feminine and more delightful than Sophia.

§

Dr. Leavis, after dismissing *Tom Jones* on the ground that Fielding's attitudes and his concern with human nature are so simple that they must produce the effect of monotony on a mature mind, asserts that 'what he *can* do appears to best effect in *Joseph Andrews* . . . and by *Amelia* he has gone soft'. What exactly he means by this criticism of *Amelia* is not evident, though it is plainly derogatory.

Soft in his presentation of human life in *Amelia* Fielding assuredly is not. The background – the trading justices, the debtors' prisons and sponging houses, the cynicism and corruption of high society, 'the spurns that patient merit of the unworthy takes' – is rendered with a steady realism. Perhaps Dr. Leavis means that Fielding is 'soft' – in a different sense – in his attitude towards Amelia and Booth, because he depicts Amelia as tender, affectionate and forgiving to an extreme, and her husband as exasperatingly weak on crucial occasions. But this, surely, is not softness in Fielding – not in any reprehensible sense, anyhow. Both Amelia and Booth are eminently credible. Indeed, the queer thing about Amelia is that, although abstractly considered she is a paragon of wifely affection, she is also a perfectly individual human being, whom Fielding presents with a sort of candour and simplicity that in retrospect seems almost magical. For instance, when Booth's suspicions of the noble lord's intentions toward Amelia have been aroused by Colonel James, and he cannot refrain from hinting them to her, while they lie awake in bed, he is overcome and silenced by her obvious inability to imagine evil: which moves him, as well it might, to loving admiration.

'Well but', said she smiling, 'do confess, my dear, the truth; I promise I won't blame you nor disesteem you for it; but is not pride really at the bottom of this fear of an obligation?'

'Perhaps it may', answered he; 'or, if you will, you may call it fear. I own I am afraid of obligations, as the worst kind of debts; for I have generally observed those who confer them expect to be repaid ten thousand-fold.'

Here ended all that is material of their discourse; and a little time afterwards they both fell asleep in each other's arms; from which time Booth had no more restlessness, nor any further perturbation in his dreams.

Is that 'soft', or is Fielding 'soft' for writing it? A great many of his contemporary readers thought so, though the word they used was 'insipid'. Were they right or wrong? I think, utterly wrong. At any rate, *Amelia* as a novel ultimately must stand or fall by the tone of such a passage: for it pervades the whole of the book. And it is quite deliberate. Fielding fully means to say what he is saying there, and to say it in exactly that way. The title of the chapter is: *Which will not appear, we presume, unnatural to all married readers*. The emphasis is on 'all'. There is, Fielding implies and believes, at least a saving remnant of wives and husbands who have experienced the reality of married love.

That and nothing else is the true subject of *Amelia*. Just as in *Tom Jones* the attainment of possession of the beloved woman by the faithful lover is represented as the *summum bonum*, so in *Amelia* the continuance of love in the married state is represented as the necessary consequence of authentic pre-marital love, and as the supreme felicity. This it is that sustains Amelia and Booth amid their misfortunes, guards them against despair, and is the thread of gold in the sordid texture of society. But whereas in the earlier novel Tom's lapses with Molly and Mrs. Waters and the Bellaston are plausibly represented in some sort as venial, and indeed as so many vagaries of a good nature denied its proper anchorage

in the grounded hope that Sophia will marry him, in *Amelia*
Booth's affair with Miss Matthews must of necessity be a real
infidelity. Fielding does all in his power to mitigate it. It comes
at the end of a long and subtle scene which lasts for three
books – one quarter of the whole novel – wherein Booth, on
the one side, comes to realize that he has been unconsciously
Miss Matthews' first and enduring love, while she, on the
other, has her passion inflamed by Booth's description of his
love for Amelia. Even so, the amour comes with a shock: but
with the kind of shock that Fielding is so expert in inflicting,
which makes us say: 'Alas, this is only too natural in the
circumstances.' There was perhaps no need for Fielding to
restate the defence:

> We desire, therefore, the good-natured and candid reader
> will be pleased to weigh attentively the several unlucky
> circumstances which concurred so critically, that Fortune
> seemed to have used her utmost endeavours to ensnare
> poor Booth's constancy. Let the reader set before his eyes a
> fine young woman, in a manner a first love, conferring
> obligations and using every art to soften, to allure, to win
> and to enflame; let him consider the time and place; let
> him remember that Mr. Booth was a young fellow in the
> highest vigour of life; and, lastly, let him add one
> single circumstance, that the parties were alone to-
> gether; and then, if he will not acquit the defendant,
> he must be convicted, for I have no more to say in his
> defence.

In fact, Fielding has already said a good deal more, when
Booth ends his own story to Miss Matthews with telling of his
arrest and his committal

'. . . hither; where I should probably have starved, had I not from your hands found a most unaccountable preservation. – And here, give me leave to assure you, my dear Miss Matthews, that, whatever advantage, I may have reaped from your misfortune, I sincerely lament it; nor would I have purchased any relief to myself at the price of seeing you in this deadful place.'

He spake these last words with great tenderness; for he was a man of consummate good nature, and had formerly had much affection for this young lady: indeed, more than the generality of people are capable of entertaining for any person whatsoever.

That is Fielding's essential defence of Booth's infidelity. The good-natured man is rare, and his genuine tenderness by its rarity arouses in an unhappy woman a passionate response, to which he in turn cannot refuse to respond without some sense of guilt. The Bellaston's affair with Tom Jones has a tinge of this redeeming grace. In Booth's affair with Miss Matthews, there is much more of it. In order that we should admit it, she is made a more attractive character than the Bellaston. Though, like her, she is vindictive when her passion is rejected, she is incapable of the Bellaston's cold and deliberate plotting of a horrible revenge; and her generosity is of a totally different order. It is spontaneous, quick and reckless: she would fling her all at the feet of the man she loves. She has imaginative sympathy too, as when she says that Booth should have accepted the twelve pounds which Atkinson offered him – 'I am convinced you hurt him very much when you refused it.' There is no reason to believe that Booth has found the secret of her when he says that vanity is her ruling passion.

If you will administer to that, [he tells Colonel James] it will infallibly throw her into your arms. To this I attribute my own unfortunate success. While she relieved my wants and distresses she was daily feeding her own vanity; whereas, as every gift of yours asserted superiority, it rather offended than pleased her.

It hardly fits the facts, though it does fit Booth's character, in that he was too devoid of self-complacency to ascribe her passion for him to its evident cause.

However that may be, Miss Matthews is a memorable portrait of a woman. Fielding simply presents her, and we believe in her reality, just as we believe in the reality of that paradoxical character, Colonel James, who became permanently infatuated by her. Booth is completely mistaken (as Miss Matthews is not) concerning James's character.

In truth, the colonel, though a very generous man, had not the least grain of tenderness in his disposition. His mind was formed of those firm materials of which nature formerly hammered out the Stoic, and upon which the sorrows of no man living could make an impression. A man of this temper, who doth not much value danger, will fight for the person he calls his friend, and the man that hath but little value for his money will give it him; but such friendship is never to be absolutely depended on, for whenever the favourite passion interposes with it, it is sure to subside and vanish into air. Whereas the man whose tender disposition really feels the miseries of another will endeavour to relieve them for his own sake; and, in such a mind, friendship will often get the superiority over every other passion.

Booth, because of the tenderness of his own good nature, entirely misinterprets the colonel's apparent generosity, thinking his acts proceed from the same motive as they would in himself: so that he absolutely refuses to believe that James is plotting to seduce Amelia, and she dares not tell him of her suspicions. On the other side, Amelia is equally credulous concerning the good intentions of the unpleasant lord, and Booth dares not be explicit about his suspicions. The situation, as it develops between them, is truly subtle; yet it is, as ever, quite simply presented, with a minimum of psychologization, with the effect that, however much we deplore some of Booth's weaknesses, we become increasingly convinced that these two creatures, so alike in their congenital incapacity for thinking evil, are really made for each other. Booth's innocence is tarnished, indeed, compared to Amelia's, but it is essentially uncorrupt. They can trust each other. And the dramatic suspense and pathos of the novel lies mainly in the fact that Booth has a guilty secret that he dares not confess. When, in his final catastrophe, he makes a clean breast of his infidelity, and he and we, with equal surprise, learn that Amelia knows all about it, and has forgiven him long ago, our satisfaction is whole-hearted. This, we feel, is as it should be: for this is love.

§

If this quiet, unemphatic insistence on love as a reality and as the supreme good in human life is a sign that Fielding has 'gone soft', one can only be thankful that he had the honesty and the courage to do so. Yet it is difficult to see what else Dr. Leavis can mean by his criticism of *Amelia*. It is not as though Fielding indulges in any sentimental expatiations; on the contrary he presents the revealing situations with the utmost economy, indeed more like a playwright than a novelist. We *Yes!!!* are wrought to such a pitch of sympathy with Amelia and Booth in their complex misfortunes that Booth's imprudences become absolutely harrowing: for example, when he is persuaded by the honest old lieutenant to give the £50, which Amelia has scraped up for him to repay the villainous Trent, as a bribe to 'the great man' to get himself placed on the active list. The pathos is in the bare situation. Fielding does not exploit it. If the spectacle of innocence caught in the toils of evil because of its innocence is soft, then *Othello* is soft. If *Joseph Andrews* represents what Fielding can do, and *Amelia* is (as Dr. Leavis implies) an almost weak-minded exhibition of what he cannot do, one longs to be vouchsafed some explanation of what, in fact, Fielding has achieved in *Amelia*. It really is not nothing.

If we try to get some illumination on Dr. Leavis's strange judgments, by asking what it is that *Joseph Andrews* positively has and *Amelia* has not, the only possible answer seems to be: comic characters and comic situations. *Amelia* has no comic situations, and only one character who is to some extent comic, in Colonel Bath. Fielding's high spirits, already perceptibly lowered in *Tom Jones*, have vanished entirely in *Amelia*. It is easy enough to assign causes to the change of temper: growing physical exhaustion, the awareness that he had not much longer to live, and a constant contact, as the Bow Street magistrate, with the miseries that lay beneath the surface of existence in London – all the experience which lay behind his forceful and fearful phrase concerning the London poor: 'They starve and freeze and rot among themselves; they rob and steal and beg among their betters.' But the change of temper brought with it no diminution of creative power: only a change of focus. The characters in *Amelia* are, if anything, more real than those in *Tom Jones*, with the exception of Tom and Sophia. Miss Matthews is more convincing than the Bellaston, Dr. Harrison than Mr. Allworthy, Atkinson than Partridge. That is not to say that the first and the last of these are more excellent creations. But evidently Fielding was much more concerned than he had been before to present a truthful picture of London society, in much the same way as he was concerned to portray the love which comes after marriage instead of that which comes before it.

Amelia is, just as certainly as *Tom Jones*, a great novel. Whether or not it is in 'the great tradition' is a minor matter. It is an absorbing story of credible and lovable human beings, whose characters and vicissitudes appeal to what is permanent in our human sympathies. If, as I believe, Dr. Johnson was right in holding that 'nothing can please many and please long but just representations of human nature', the high place of *Amelia* in the list of English novels is secure. To insinuate that it, and *Tom Jones*, are empty of interest and full of monotony for a mature mind, 'demanding more than external action', is to reckon as nugatory the rare talent which, with a minimum of elaboration, can put before the imagination characters which we can believe in and love, which endure in the memory and take their place with some of Shakespeare's as types of natural humanity.

No doubt this is a talent which cannot be learned from Fielding. He, like Shakespeare, offers little for his successors to absorb and use – except a valid criterion of what is 'a just representation of human nature'. It would be disastrous to attempt to imitate him, unless in the same limited way that he, in *Amelia*, imitated Virgil. 'The candid and learned reader will see that the latter [Virgil] was the noble model I made use of on this occasion.' So he wrote in the *Covent Garden Journal* in his defence of his last novel; he also declared that 'of all my offspring she is the favourite child'. It is curious that no critic has picked up the hint, for it is plain enough, even without it, that the technique of the long retrospective conversation between Booth and Miss Matthews in the sponging house, which occupies the first three books, is based on Aeneas's long story of Dido, and the story ends in much the same unhappy infatuation. This classical structure might conceivably be adapted again with equal effect. But it would be much more difficult for any novelist to make use of the distinctive patterns of close-packed, lucid, sub-ironic dialogue which Fielding so frequently employs – for example, in *Joseph Andrews*, between Lady Booby and Joseph, and in *Tom Jones* between the Bellaston and Sophia – and altogether impossible for him to imitate Fielding's method of making his characters live, and so ordering them and their relations as to convince us, as it were by simple inspection, that the one thing needful is the goodness of nature which alone bestows the capacity for love.

That is inimitable, chiefly because it is impossible to discover precisely how Fielding does it. We are reduced to simply registering the fact that, as Coleridge said: 'By no writer was the momentous distinction between character and conduct, between being and doing so finely brought forward as by Fielding.' It was his natural and peculiar genius to be able to do precisely this thing. Probably, it was his instinctive recoil from the false morality of *Pamela* that made him conscious of his talent and his task, and brought him to the knowledge of what was to be done: for there is singularly little trace of any attempt towards it in the long sequence of his plays. But he discovered his true bent just in time to produce a trilogy of novels that are sane and sound and true. And it will not do to argue (as Dr. Leavis does) that Coleridge's judgment is obsolete, because there were so few novels in his time with which to compare Fielding's. How many novels since Coleridge's time have surpassed Fielding's in their own specific excellence – of demonstrating, by making visible through credible created characters, the moral distinction which Coleridge justly called momentous? Even the greatest Victorian novelists were compelled to run in blinkers round the fundamental question of sex-morality. Who, for example, can do more than vaguely guess at the true sex-relation between Gwendolen and Grandcourt in *Daniel Deronda*? Yet it is obviously crucial, and largely because of the reticence Grandcourt becomes an unreal and unnatural figure beside such a character as Fielding's Colonel James. There is a real substance in Thackeray's lament that since Fielding, no novelist had dared to portray a man. And now when the freedom has been regained, the novelty of the condition seems to have produced an excess and a cynicism which are as unnatural as the former reticence.

§

One may admit, without any reluctance, that Fielding's sense of form is, by the standards of subsequent achievement, defective. His prefaces, his long interludes, and his innumerable minor digressions would be better out of the way, though it is obvious that he was feeling his way to greater self-discipline. The proportion of unnecessary material is much smaller in *Amelia* than in the previous books. And, in any case, the prefaces are to be understood not only as an effort to beguile and resharpen the appetite of the reader of a long narrative, but equally as the attempt of a conscious but tentative innovator to explain what he is about. But, in spite of these approximations and encumbrances, he succeeds magnificently in his main purpose: to present us with human beings who are real and natural, with whose vicissitudes we deeply sympathize, and to present them so that they exhibit a system of moral values which we, having had our minds cleared of cant by Fielding himself, recognize to be sound. Dr. Leavis singles out, as the characteristic marks of the great English novelists, from whose company he so peremptorily extrudes Fielding, that 'they are all distinguished by a vital capacity for experience, a kind of reverent openness before life, and a marked moral intensity'. But in all these qualities Fielding is conspicuous; and in respect of the last he is hardly less in advance of this age than he was of his own. The trouble is that Fielding's kind of moral intensity, not being laboured, does not lend itself to laborious analysis and critical expatiation. For that reason it can, apparently, pass entirely unrecognized: dismissed as 'the genial tolerance of the man-about-town', or as 'a simple attitude'. Nevertheless, it exists and is pervasive. And those who are sensitive to it and care to investigate the ethical thinking on which it was based, or by which it was confirmed, may find it in an unexpected place: the long essay which Fielding wrote in 1740, entitled *An Apology for the Clergy*.

There is some irony in this admirable essay, which is ostensibly designed to counter that contempt for the clergy of which Fielding gives a vivid picture in the Vauxhall scene of

Amelia. That contempt, he says, is due to the ignorance of the character of a clergyman.

> Such ignorance I shall attempt to remove: since I do not recollect any modern writings tending that way, and it may require some reflection and parts to collect a true idea of so amiable a character from nice observations on the general behaviour of the clergy.

But the irony is a prelude to a remarkable analysis of the Christian character, based indeed on St. Paul's eulogy of Love in 1 Cor. xiii, but showing plainly that Fielding had thought long and hard about St. Paul's conception, with the Greek text before his eyes, or his memory. His expansion of the apostle's meaning, article by article, into a *vade mecum* is simple, illuminating and persuasive. Thus, for example, it expounds 'rejoicing in the truth' into 'delighting in the company of good and virtuous men, regardless of their wealth'; and 'believing all things, hoping all things' into 'weighing all mankind in the scales of friendship and seeing them with the eyes of love'. He sums up the character accordingly, and concludes that 'a bad clergyman is the worst of men' because, 'if not an idiot, he *must* be an unbeliever, and a hypocrite'.

Such is the ethical and religious ideal which animates his creation of clerical characters in his novels, beginning with the chaplain of Newgate in *Jonathan Wild*. The variety of them is almost as great in Fielding as it is in George Eliot; and the space they occupy in Fielding's fiction is proportionately greater. Unlike George Eliot, whose clergymen, with one exception, are all men in whom the good predominates, and whose presence enriches their parish or their congregation, Fielding presents a majority of bad or indifferent ones: the Newgate chaplain; Barnabas and Trulliber; Thwackum; the young clerical prig who disputes with Dr. Harrison, and Miss Bennet's father who lapses into infatuation and domestic tyranny. But these are set against the shining examples of Parson Adams and Dr. Harrison himself. Methodism, Evangelicalism and the Oxford Movement had intervened between the two great novelists, and we may suppose that Fielding's picture was as true for his day as George Eliot's was for a century later. Those who lazily cherish the conventional picture of harum-scarum Harry Fielding, and find difficulty in admitting to their minds that he was so seriously occupied with the Christian character as his novels indicate, should read *An Apology for the Clergy*, which preceded them all.

They will then realize on what a deep well of moral conviction Fielding drew for the sustenance of his fiction. He believed that Christian love and human friendship and the love between man and woman were intimately allied by the tenderness they had in common; he believed, too, that this tenderness could impart a grace even to a casual sex-relation; he believed that there was a generosity of the body. Tenderness, warmth, sympathy, gratitude, generosity were the true virtues; cruelty, coldness, hardness, hypocrisy, ungratefulness, meanness the true vices. Self-regarding egoism, no matter what uniform of respectability it carried, was hateful; solicitude for others, no matter how disreputably arrayed, was to be loved. With what some may think a reprehensible lack of supernatural reference, he made his own the injunction: *Ama, et fac quod vis*. The same critics may charge him with confusing eros and agape, though in fact he was simply and directly aware of the realm where they are congruent. Of that city he was a citizen: and who shall say it is not the city of God? Love was a dimension of experience which was a familiar and domestic reality to him: the infallible solvent of all bitterness. Although it sharpened his awareness of how

> Man, proud man,
> Dressed in a little brief authority,
> Plays such fantastic tricks before high heaven
> As make the angels weep;

it enabled him, for all his anger and indignation, to laugh and remain a happy man.

Clare Revisited

Clare Revisited

★

IT is high time he was, by me. It is sobering to think thirty-five years have passed since I first met Edmund Blunden – at Garsington under the generous (and now almost legendary) wing of Lady Ottoline Morrell – and he, instead of speaking of himself as I had hoped, talked with eager and contagious enthusiasm of the many unpublished poems of John Clare which he had recently tracked down. Until that moment Clare was hardly more than a name to me. Shortly afterwards he presented me with a whole series of beautifully written transcripts of his discoveries. I was instantly converted, and I tried to repay a little of my obligation to him by finding a publisher for the poems he had recovered, and writing an essay upon them.

All that, as I say, was thirty-five years ago. Much has been done for Clare since then: first and foremost, by Mr. Blunden himself, who published more of Clare's poetry and prose and, in his account of *Keats's Publisher*, shed new illumination on Clare's life; next by Professor and Mrs. Tibble who wrote an admirable life of Clare and then published the completest editions of Clare's poems and prose so far; and finally by Mr. Geoffrey Grigson, who first edited anew the *Poems of John Clare's Madness* and prefaced them with a penetrating introductory essay, and then compiled the best anthology of Clare's poetry with yet another admirable preface. It is through the devoted labours of all these that I have been enabled to revisit a somewhat different, and even more exciting Clare; and I am duly grateful.

I

I have been struck by two main deficiencies in my ancient appreciation of Clare, from which, as far as it goes, I have nothing to withdraw. These deficiencies are of quite different orders. The less important was that I did not realize how precious and unique was the picture of the effects of enclosure which Clare has left to posterity. The more important was that I did insufficient justice to the power of Clare as a visionary poet – that is to say, a poet of experience outside the familiar range of our experience, and incommensurable with it. The group of his poems which fall within the category is a small one, and they were written during the early years of his madness. Most of them appear to have been written in or about 1844; one is dated 1847, after which Clare's sudden access of the power of intense concentration, emotional and intellectual seems to have left him. He wrote many charming things; but they became slighter and slighter; and very few of them reached the level of the copious best of his pre-asylum work. The wonderful freshness of perception disappears. What remains is his native facility in rhyming, ennobled by rare flashes of the old vividness.

Roughly speaking, what confronts us is the phenomenon of a poet of unique though limited achievement who, under the stress of the threatening disintegration of his personality, suddenly becomes the vehicle for the utterance of thoughts hitherto beyond the reaches of his soul, of terrors and triumphs which belong to the struggle to maintain the integrity of the human personality against the powers that would engulf it. Nothing in Clare's pre-asylum poetry has prepared us for quite this kind of intensity. He has passed into a new dimension of experience.

Certainly the most famous, and probably the finest, of these visionary poems is the one entitled *A Vision*. It is dated August 2, 1844.

> I lost the love of heaven above,
>   I spurned the lust of earth below,
> I felt the sweets of fancied love,
>   And hell itself my only foe.
>
> I lost earth's joys, but felt the glow
>   Of heaven's flame abound in me,
> Till loveliness and I did grow
>   The bard of immortality.
>
> I loved but woman fell away
>   I hid me from the faded flame,[1]
> I snatch'd the sun's eternal ray
>   And wrote till earth was but a name.
>
> In every language upon earth,
>   On every shore, o'er every sea,
> I gave my name immortal birth
>   And kept my spirit with the free.

[1] Mr. Grigson prints 'fame'; but since Mr. and Mrs. Tibble still print 'flame', and I am not qualified to judge between these authorities I retain the reading which is familiar to me.

That stands, by the most rigorous judgment, equal with some of the finest of Blake. And it is almost equally mysterious. What is plain about it is that it is a song of spiritual triumph. It celebrates, in itself embodies and eternizes, a moment of victory: at once, spiritual and poetic. Clare, for this creative instant, has fought free of the powers of darkness, and is himself: a new self, deepened and purified by the struggle he has endured. And this new and deeper self is a self of pure poetry. For, almost from the beginning, Clare had experienced his own essence as poetry. The rapture of his heightened perceptions had uttered itself immediately in rhyme. This natural song, shaped upon whatever patterns he could find, had been the mode of his real, or most essential and personal existence: the speech of his own reality, of the love which was for him the mode of true being.

Poets love nature, and themselves are love.

In this sense, it was inevitable that the achievement of a deeper, purer self, torn free from the powers of disintegration, and momentarily triumphant over them, should be the achievement of a poem of a new and higher order. *A Vision is* Clare's victory.

But, on a rather lower level, we may fairly ask: What does the poem mean? There is one important clue in Clare's earlier poetry: in the opening lines of *The Village Minstrel*, written at Helpstone about 1819.

> While learned poets rush to bold extremes,
> And sunbeams snatch to light the muse's fires,
> An humble rustic hums his lowly dreams,
> Far in the swale where poverty retires,
> And sings what nature and what truth inspires.

In *A Vision* Clare himself has become 'a learned poet rushing to bold extremes', and more. But the humbler lines are a complete commentary on the pride and splendour of

> I snatch'd the sun's eternal ray
> And wrote till earth was but a name.

The writing he meant was the writing of that poem and no other; his former poetry of earth, in the writing of that poem, was dissolved away. And indeed it was. He had, and knew he had, fought his way to the pinnacle. He was there. He was himself, *dans sa vraie vérité*.

Then the hyperbole of the last verse, beginning: 'In every language upon earth . . .' It is not fanciful, nor pedestrian, to connect this with one of Clare's hallucinations. 'When . . . I courted your mother, I knew nine languages', he wrote to his son from the asylum, but, he explained, he kept them to himself, and only betrayed his knowledge in conversation with parsons and gentry. The knowledge of many languages belonged, for Clare, to the free-masonry of the learned, who as poets 'snatched sunbeams'. It had been part of his secret endowment; now, having climbed the pinnacle, he proclaims it.

Again, the last two lines:

> I gave my name immortal birth
> And kept my spirit with the free.

What does the last line mean? Probably, more things than one. That he kept, in spite of his prison and the inward assaults upon his own identity, his essential liberty – the spiritual liberty of which the poem is the utterance. That he, having become, with loveliness, 'the bard of immortality', joined the free on the heights of eternal song. These meanings are there. But there is surely another. In one of his later songs he writes, of the raindrops:

> They come from heaven and there the Free
> Sends down his blessings upon me;

and in another he writes of flowers:

> Even in prison they can solace me
> For where they bloom God is, and I am free.

In the concluding lines of the impressive piece *Written in a Thunderstorm* (1841), he had besought the elements:

> Bid the earth and its delusions pass away
> But leave the mind, as its Creator, free.

And there is the lovely end of *The Dying Child*:

> His soul seemed with the free,
> He died so quietly.

To be with the free, evidently, also meant for Clare to be one with God, as he conceived God. A further link between these meanings is supplied by another of his visionary poems: usually entitled *John Clare*.

> I feel I am, I only know I am
>   And plod upon the earth as dull and void:
> Earth's prison chilled my body with its dram
>   Of dullness and my soaring thoughts destroyed.
> I fled to solitudes from passion's dream,
>   But strife pursued – I only know I am.

Clare Revisited

I was a being created in the race
  Of men, disdaining bounds of place and time,
A spirit that could travel o'er the space
  Of earth and heaven, like a thought sublime,
Tracing creation – like my Maker, free, –
  A soul unshackled – like eternity,
Spurning earth's vain and soul-debasing thrall –
But now I only know I am, – that's all.

It is possible, even probable, that this was written after
A Vision, and represents a moment of awareness that he had
fallen from that visionary pinnacle, yet one of sufficient
control to enable him to express, at least in part, what he had
won and lost. Anyway, I do not believe that the condition
described in 'I was a being . . .' is the condition of his pre-
asylum days, of the incessant composition of nature poetry.
Or, at least, it is that condition transfigured by a subsequent
flash of insight. Clare did not, in the earlier days, conceive or
experience himself as like 'a thought sublime, tracing creation'.
That fine phrase belongs to a different order of self-knowledge.
The new thrilling and perilous dimension has broken in,
wherein he is, or had been, one with God: consubstantial and
co-eternal with his Creator. And that is the deepest meaning
of the phrase: 'I kept my spirit with the free.'

It is not that the description of what he was is, in essence,
false to what he had actually been. Clare's condition, as the
maker of spontaneous and incessant poetry of nature, with its
continual breath-taking revelation of simple things as they are,
sub specie aeternitatis, recalls Keats's description of the soul
of a child as it enters the world, which is the vale of soul-
making.

There may be intelligences or sparks of the divinity in millions – but they are not souls till they acquire identities, till each one is personally itself. Intelligences are atoms of perception – they know and they see and they are pure, in short they are God.

To apply this simple and profound terminology to the growth of his poetic nature, the pre-asylum Clare was an unconscious atom of God. His perilous triumph, won at the cost of an imminent disintegration of his personal identity, was the flash of the knowledge that he was one with God. There is nothing exorbitant in this. It is a familiar realization of the mystic experience. And Clare's sudden illumination transfigured his own poetic past, and revealed to him his own meaning as a poet, as it were in a lightning flash.

This peculiar transfiguration of his own past is almost palpable in another of this group of poems.

> I hid my love when young till I
> Couldn't bear the buzzing of a fly;
> I hid my love to my despite
> Till I could not bear to look at light:
> I dare not gaze upon her face
> But left her memory in each place;
> Where'er I saw a wild flower lie
> I kissed and bade my love good-bye.
>
> I met her in the greenest dells,
> Where dewdrops pearl the wood blue-bells;
> The lost breeze kissed her bright blue eye,
> The bee kissed and went singing by,

Clare Revisited

A sunbeam found a passage there,
A gold chain round her neck so fair
As secret as the wild bee's song
She lay there all the summer long.

I hid my love in field and town
Till e'en the breeze would knock me down;
The bees seemed singing ballads o'er,
The fly's bass turned a lion's roar;
And even silence found a tongue
To haunt me all the summer long.
The riddle nature could not prove
Was nothing else but secret love.

That is not remembered experience; it is a germ of past experience unfolded in a new dimension, under the compulsion of a new significance, when he has learned that the love he cherished as a boy was the spark of the flame of an awful power which he has felt in all its might. That power he projects into the past. It is a moment of intense vision, related to that general transfiguration of Mary Joyce, his childish sweetheart, into a symbol of freedom, of poetry, of love, of childhood felicity, of unattainable peace, and also of life's treachery, and woman's falsehood, which is diffused throughout his later poetry. But the peculiar power of this poem derives from the injection of his present experience into the past: like an electric current of high voltage poured into the filament of a dim lamp, which will either burn it out or create a startling incandescence.

That brings us back to *A Vision*. His victory there is in some sense a passing beyond the love of woman, which has failed him.

> I loved, but woman fell away,
> I hid me from her faded flame.

This connects with the lines from *I am*:

> I fled to solitudes from passion's dream
> But strife pursued.

In *A Vision* he is beyond that strife, which is a word he often uses in his 'mad' poems for the mental conflict which seethed in him between the past and the present, between darkness and illumination, between hope and despair, and above all between the knowledge that his love of Mary had been doomed long ago, and the hope of possessing her presence for ever. This mental tumult is described and transcended in the opening lines of *A Vision* –

> I lost the love of heaven above
> I spurned the lust of earth below
> I felt the joys of fancied love,
> And hell itself my only foe. –

where, it seems, the heavenly love lost is his childhood love of Mary, and the fancied love was his dream of being married to her, threatened by the terrors of his 'dark and fathomless' mind. He is where he longs to be in *I am*:

> I long for scenes, where man hath never trod,
> A place where woman never smiled or wept . . .

But in two beautiful poems of this group, Mary is the companion of his purified spirit. *Invite to Eternity* is an extraordinary achievement. It appears to have originated in a

64

moment when he was able to accept the disintegration of his personality and to see in that very condition an opening of the gate to eternity – a strange eternity where Mary may be his veiled companion.

> Say, maiden, wilt thou go with me,
> In this strange death of life to be,
> To live in death and be the same
> Without this life, or home, or name,
> At once to be and not to be –
> That was and is not – yet to see
> Things pass like shadows, and the sky
> Above, below, around us lie?
>
> The land of shadows wilt thou trace
> And look – nor know each other's face;
> The present marred[1] with reason gone
> And past and present all as one?
> Say, maiden, can thy life be led
> To join the living with the dead?
> Then trace thy footsteps on with me;
> We're wed to one eternity,

[1] Here Mr. Grigson prints 'mixed' for 'marred'. But Mr. and Mrs. Tibble print 'marred', to which I have been accustomed. It is in accord with Clare's attitude to 'reason' elsewhere: e.g. in *The Shepherd's Calendar:*

> Where are they gone – the joys and fears
> The links, the life of other years?
> I thought they twined about my heart
> So close, that we could never part.
> But Reason, like a winter's day,
> Nipp'd childhood's visions all away –

where Reason has destroyed the continuity of the past with the present, as in *Invite*.

It haunts the mind and will not be forgotten. The pathos of the condition of 'sad non-identity' has never received more perfect utterance.

It is the Evening Hour is simpler and slighter, but very lovely. The Mary of reality was blue-eyed; this is the transfigured presence.

> Spirit of her I love
>   Whispering to me
> Stories of sweet visions, as I rove,
>   Here stop and crop with me
> Sweet flowers that in the still hour grew,
> We'll take them home, nor shake off the bright dew.
>
> Mary, or sweet spirit of thee,
>   As the bright sun shines tomorrow,
> Thy dark eyes these flowers shall see
>   Gathered by me in sorrow,
> In the still hour when my mind was free
> To walk alone – yet wish I walked with thee.

As it is – at any rate for me – impossible to say whether *A Vision* or *Invite to Eternity* is the finer poem, so it is impossible to say which of the two very different conditions of mind, or states of soul, which they express, is the higher. *A Vision* is excited, *Invite* is calm. 'Beyond woman' was a position hard for Clare to attain, and the tension of struggle is in *A Vision*: it bears the marks of scars. The sad lucidity of *Invite* is serene. They embody different, but equally astonishing victories of the poetic spirit over disaster.

Clare Revisited

§

These poems were written round about 1844, three years after Clare's entry in Northampton Asylum, where he remained until his death in 1864. Clare's previous history, in so far as it is immediately relevant to the condition in which he produced these poems, may be briefly told. In 1832 he had moved from his native village of Helpstone to a small holding at Northborough three miles away, with the hope of achieving independence. The initial success of his poetry had not been sustained, and his just hopes of independence through his poetry were disappointed. He was a prey to fits of extreme depression. But, though he was at first unhappy at Northborough, he wrote there much of his most beautiful nature poetry. By stages which the available evidence does not permit us to follow, his mental condition became acute after five years, and in June, 1837 he was placed under the care of Dr. Allen, a remarkably enlightened alienist, in his private establishment at Epping. There he remained, suffering from strange delusions as to his personal identity, till July, 1841, when he was overcome by a longing to return to Northborough. He made his way home on foot, and practically without food, in four days, with the pathetic expectation of finding Mary, to whom he now believed he was married. Actually, Mary had been dead three years; and in any case Clare had not even seen her for twenty-five years. But he had written her a letter, as to his wife, from Epping, which alternates between indignation with her for not having come to see him, and affection for her and his imaginary children by her. After five months at home he was certified as insane and taken on December 29, 1841 to Northampton Asylum, where he remained until his death.

During his sojourn at Epping he wrote little poetry. It included one lovely piece, which begins

> No single hour can stand for naught
> No moment-hand can move
> But calendars an aching thought
> Of my first lonely love.

and the powerful verses *Written in a Thunderstorm, July 15, 1841* – that is, a week before his escape – which end:

> I live in love, sun of undying light
> And fathom my own heart for ways of good;
> In its pure atmosphere, day without night
> Smiles on the plains, the forest and the flood.
>
> Smile on, ye elements of earth and sky,
> Or frown in thunders as ye frown on me.
> Bid earth and its delusions pass away
> But leave the mind as its creator free.

Previous to this, in the persuasion that he was Byron, he had begun two Byronic poems: *Don Juan* and *Child Harold*. *Don Juan* is interesting chiefly as showing the sexual starvation from which he suffered in his seclusion at Epping. Its poetic merits are dim. The assumption of cynicism did not sit well on Clare, whose longing for the comfort of physical love was innocent and natural.

> Lord bless me, now the day is in the gloaming
>   And every evil thought is out of sight
> How should I like to purchase some sweet woman
>   Or else creep in with my two wives tonight –
> Surely that wedding day is on the coming.

Clare Revisited

Absence, like physic, poisons all delight.
Mary and Martha, both an evil omen,
Though both my own – they still belong to no men.

Curiously enough, Mary Joyce and Martha Turner ('Patty', whom he actually married) did occupy something like their legendary and symbolic places in Clare's private universe. Martha was certainly 'cumbered about with many cares', while Mary, in the main, was the ideal love, who listened to his poetry and shared his perceptions.

In *Child Harold*, which is a document of crucial importance for the understanding of Clare's condition and contains scattered passages of great pathos and poetic power, he is explicit about the function of the transfigured Mary.

Mary, thou ace of hearts, thou muse of song,
  The pole-star of my being and decay . . .
Mary, thy name loved long still keeps me free
Till my lost life becomes a part of thee.

Love is the mainspring of existence – It
  Becomes a soul whereby I live to love.
On all I see that dearest name is writ.
  Falsehood is here – but truth has life above
  Where every star that shines exists in love.
Skies vary in their clouds – the seasons vary
  From heat to cold. Change cannot constant prove.
The south is bright, but smiles can act contrary –
My guide star gilds the north – and shines with Mary.

My life hath been one love – no, blot it out –
  My life hath been one chain of contradictions –
Madhouses, prisons, whoreshops – never doubt
  But that my life hath had some strong convictions
  That such was wrong. Religion makes restrictions.
I would have followed, but life turned a bubble
And clomb the giant stile of maledictions.
They took me from my wife and to save trouble
I wed again, and made the error double.

To that conception of his love-life the quivering needle of
Clare's splintered mind constantly returned. But it quivered
wildly. At times he believed that all his mortal loves had
betrayed him (as in *Don Juan*); at times, as here, it was the
powers of evil who, by taking Mary from him, forced him
into evil ways. At yet other times, he rejoiced that possession
of Mary had been denied him, and that, having been spared the
inevitable disillusion of reality, he was free to make her the
symbol of poetry and love and truth and peace.

Whatever Clare's life may have been, certainly his poem
Child Harold is a chain of contradictions. Few consecutive
stanzas are as coherent as those quoted above; and its fundamental contradictions are almost absolute. The alternations
between faith in Mary and accusations of her faithlessness,
between acknowledgment of his final separation from her and
belief in some kind of reunion, between seeking rest in utter
solitude and longing for woman's companionship, are incessant. At one bewildering moment quite another woman,
'sweet Bessey' (who may be either of two Elizabeths known in
Clare's life), makes a sudden appearance. Now, the release of
death is longed for; now, dreaded as the beginning of eternal

grief. At other times, as in four stanzas on the miseries of orphanhood, a quite distinct and entirely irrelevant theme is introduced. At one moment Clare seems to have been fully conscious of his incoherence.

> Flow on, my verse, though barren thou mayst be
>   Of thought – yet sing and let thy fancies roll!
> In early days thou swept a mighty sea,
>   All calm in troublous deeps, and spurned control.
>   Thou fire and iceberg to an aching soul
> And still an angel in my gloomy way,
>   Far better opiate than the draining bowl,
> Still sing, my muse, to drive care's fiends away
> Nor heed what loitering listener hears the lay.

That was, no doubt, the true motive to this saddening poem. In adding verse to verse, probably at long intervals (for only occasionally would the power of writing a verse or two come to him) he found a temporary release from his own mental incoherence.

Occasionally, he achieves a direct and memorable utterance of his mental agony.

> My mind is dark and fathomless and wears
>   The hues of hopeless agony and hell.
> No plummet ever sounds the soul's affairs:
>   There Death eternal never sounds the knell,
>   There Love imprisoned sighs the long farewell,
> And still may sigh in thoughts no heart hath penned,
>   Alone in loneliness where sorrows dwell
> And hopeless hope hopes on and meets no end –
> Wastes without springs, and homes without a friend.

Or this, with its delusion concerning the cause of the waning of his popularity:

> Fame blazed upon me with a comet's glare,
>   Fame waned and left me like a fallen star,
> Because I told the evil what they are
>   And truth and falsehood never wished to mar.
>   My life hath been a wreck, and I've gone far
> For peace and truth – and hope – for home and rest.
>   Like Eden's gates, fate throws a constant bar –
> Thoughts may o'ertake the sunset in the west:
> – Man meets no home within a woman's breast.

But, though Clare found a precious relief in continuing to write, it was plainly impossible for him to write a sustained poem, *Child Harold* is largely a series of separate and abortive poems, in most of which, no matter where he starts, he returns to the theme of love and Mary. Sometimes he expresses this with both simplicity and profundity.

> A soul within the heart that loves the more,
>   Giving to pains and fears eternal life,
> Burning the flesh till it consumes the core –
>   So Love is still the eternal calm of strife.
>   Thou soul within a soul, thou life of life,
> Thou essence of my hopes and fears and joys,
>   Mary, my first dear love and early wife,
> And still the flower my inmost soul enjoys,
> Thy love's the bloom no canker-worm destroys.

There, I think he meant that in the moments when peace descended upon his troubled and warring mind, he experienced it as love, and therefore as the spirit and presence of Mary. The flesh which this love consumes to the core is not the lust of the flesh, but what he had called 'earth's delusions' in the *Thunderstorm* lines, more or less exactly what Blake in the prophetic books meant by Vala, the realm where love, being imperfect, was tortured by jealousy. To this realm belonged Clare's upbraiding of Mary for faithlessness and betrayal. At such a moment as he records in this verse Clare felt that this was a veil of delusion which was burned away. The sense of eternal life, which is love, emerges as the still, untroubled centre within the storm of his hopes and fears. (The line in question does not mean that his hopes and fears are made eternal.)

This is only a passing moment of serenity, though there are others in the poem. But for the most part it moves within the realm of delusion. So that the theme of 'Mary' is fragmented and precarious. Sometimes, it seems to be literally true that (as he says many times in his poems) the mere word, Mary, devoid for the moment of all content, operated as a word of power upon him, a talisman bringing an assurance of his own personal identity; in the same fashion as, throughout the history of Christianity, from St. Paul onwards, the utterance of the mere name Jesus, has brought to some a sense of salvation and security. But, at this period of Clare's mental disease, Mary, as image, idea, or memory, is as incoherent as any other of his thoughts.

> Remind me not of other years, or tell
> My broken hopes of joys they are to meet,
> While thy own falsehood rings the loudest knell
> To one fond heart that aches too cold to beat.

Mary, how oft with fondness I repeat
That name alone to give my troubles rest.
The very sound, though bitter, seemeth sweet –
In my love's home and thy own faithless breast
Truth's bonds are broke and every nerve distrest.

There is the terrible paradox of Clare's mental agony – the
condition in which 'hopeless hope hopes on and meets no
end.'

It seems to Clare that the actual Mary, by not reciprocating
his youthful love, is the cause of his wrecked life. But 'Mary'
is also the genius of his childhood, which appears to him as a
paradise from which he has been cast out. So that his lost life
is in her keeping, or her spirit's. Since the main burden of his
poetry has been, and still is, regret for the vanished past – of
innocence and love and freedom – she is thus also his inspiration and his Muse: 'thou muse of song' . . . 'Mary, the Muse
of every song I write.' And since it is mainly by his effort to
go on writing poetry that he maintains some sense of his own
continuous identity, 'Mary' is indeed his salvation, his guardian
angel contending for him against the powers of darkness that
assail him. The symbol-image is ambivalent. 'Mary' is at once
his destroyer and his saviour. In the last two lines of *Child
Harold* (or the lines that are printed last: for the true order is
doubtful) are concentrated the emotional flux and reflux
which moves in the depths of the poem.

The strongest, bitterest thing that life can prove
Is woman's undisguise of hate and love.

Clare Revisited

§

We are tempted to try to delve a little further into the genesis and significance of the 'Mary' symbol for Clare. Again, one may invoke Keats by way of criterion, or rather 'control', as the word is used in experimental science. For Clare's 'Mary' has much of the mysterious ambiguity of Keats's Lamia. The difference is that Keats had the power, the poetic control, to project his inward perplexity into an objective creation. Fanny Brawne – or her potency for Keats – was transformed into the Lamia; but Clare's Mary was transfigured only into 'Mary'. In one case the cord was severed and the creation freed of entanglement in Keats's subjectivity; in the other the entanglement remains. Perhaps the thin line which divides poetic sanity from poetic madness runs here. Perhaps, too, the condition of maintaining sanity against the inevitable assaults delivered through the poet's 'more than usual organic sensibility' is to possess the power of consciously submitting with 'a wise passiveness' to that constant annihilation of the poet's identity of which Keats so often spoke – of achieving and maintaining a submissiveness towards even shattering experience which allows the self to be overborne without any tense struggle to maintain its own identity.

This may be mere speculation. But there does appear to be some connection, which is partly causal, between the one weakness of Clare's pre-asylum poetry as discerned by Keats (who appreciated Clare's positive qualities) and the final submergence of Clare's personality. Taylor wrote to Clare on Keats's behalf on September 27, 1820, when Keats had become too weak to write.

If he recovers his strength he will write to you. I think he wishes to say that your images from nature are too much introduced without being called for a particular sentiment . . . his remark is only applicable now and then when he feels as if the description overlaid and stifled that which ought to be the prevailing idea.

Keats's conception that 'a particular sentiment' or 'prevailing idea' should dominate the use of nature-imagery is closely allied to Coleridge's dictum in *Biographia Literaria*.

Images, however faithfully copied from Nature, and as accurately represented in words, do not of themselves characterize the poet. They become proofs of original genius only so far as they are modified by a predominant passion.

Coleridge's dictum is too severe, too absolute; it would deny original genius to Clare. Nature-images, of a high intensity of perception, rendered with a beautiful and deliberate precision of language, of which there are hundreds in Clare's earlier poetry, do characterize the poet. They are in themselves poetry, as Clare well knew.

A pleasing image to its page conferred,
Its living character and breathing word
Becomes a landscape, heard and felt and seen.

There are many mansions in the Father's house, and Clare, purely as a nature-poet, is secure of one. In the same way, though Clare wrote no great sonnets, as Keats did, in which the images are modified by a predominant passion, his use of a lax

sonnet form for his series of exquisite little pictures of rural life
was abundantly justified.

But it is also true that there is in Clare's poetry as a whole
an absence of that concentrated and controlling energy of
thought-feeling, which by its own authority and power
appears to evoke the reserves and residues of sensational
experience in the poet's soul and crystallize them about itself
in a sustained harmony of utterance. This deficiency may have
been due to Clare's lack of education, in the simple and
fundamental sense of training the faculty of mental concentration. His incapacity to write sustained prose points in this
direction. Very few poets have been more richly endowed with
the faculty of sheer sensuous perception: and it is understand-
able that, with his potency of sustained thought left dormant,
he should have been almost overwhelmed by the richness of
his perceptions.

Whether or not the analogy is legitimate, one feels that this
inability to subordinate his perceptions to a dominant thought-
feeling became, in the course of a life full of trials and troubles,
magnified into an incapacity to master his own moral experience. Nothing could well have been more unfortunate for one
whose intellectual fibres had not been toughened than immediate success followed by a steady dwindling of popularity.
His treatment by Taylor the publisher, too, was culpably
unimaginative and high-handed. Experiences, intoxicating and
depressing, 'came at' Clare, so to speak, with a vehemence
which a much stronger man would have had to summon up
all his reserves of fortitude to bend before and not be broken.
His first volume was published in January, 1820. It went into
four editions in a year; his next, published in 1821, just achieved
a second edition two years later; his third was not published

till 1827, and sold only 400 copies in two years. By 1829 Clare was practically unpublishable, though his production was still prolific. Nevertheless, in spite of discouragement, his poetry steadily improved. His final volume, *The Rural Muse*, published in 1835, contained much of the finest of his pre-asylum poetry, and many excellent poems were excluded from it. It is impossible to say that Clare's poetry showed any signs of the approaching catastrophe before 1835. But his behaviour seems to have done. Even as early as 1819, Drury the Stamford bookseller who introduced Clare's poetry to Taylor wrote to him:

> It is greatly to be feared that the man will be inflicted with insanity if his talent continues to be forced as it has been these four months past; he has no other mode of easing the fever that oppresses him after a tremendous fit of rhyming except by getting tipsy. A single pint of ale often does this. . . . He has rhymed and written for three days and three nights without hardly eating or sleeping.

If anybody 'forced' his talent, it was Clare himself. But the phrase is misconceived. Clare had a great natural facility, rhyming was his supreme happiness, and his beloved subject matter – Nature in all her details – was inexhaustible. That the bouts of composition were intermittent, and followed by periods of depression, emptiness and sterility, is too common a happening with poets of genius to warrant the deduction of any peculiar instability in him at the time that Drury wrote. More ominous perhaps is his own confession, two or three years later, that in the spring and the fall of every year he was visited by 'a confounded lethargy of low spirit that at times makes me feel that my sense had a mind to leave me'. Those seasons brought to him a 'weak and terrible dread and fears of dropping off'. And yet it is surely not inordinate that one so acutely sensitive to the processes of nature should have experienced a profound upheaval at the equinoxes.

On the whole it seems doubtful whether Clare's basic instability was in itself any greater than that with which other fine poets have had to contend. What he seems to have lacked, through no fault of his own, was the mental and moral stamina to humour and manage it when it was exacerbated by disappointment, financial anxiety, the responsibilities of a rapidly growing family, and intellectual isolation. This last must have been peculiarly grievous. He had grown out of village society; yet he was tied, by every fibre of his being, to the village. To create an atmosphere of friendship he drank and treated too heavily at the village inn. There was a score of £7 against him at *The Bell* in June, 1823. If these burdens could have been removed or mitigated, one feels that Clare's story might have been quite different. Perhaps Dr. Allen was over-sanguine when he said, of Clare's condition when he was first at Epping:

> I had then not the slightest hesitation in saying that if a small pension could be obtained for him, he would have recovered instantly and most probably have remained well for life.

But his opinion carries more weight than modern efforts to estimate the gravity of Clare's disease.

It is true that Clare, in the eyes of his patrons and friends, was financially secure. A fund of £375 had been raised for him in 1820, and invested at 5 per cent. The Earl Spencer allowed him £10 a year; the Marquis of Exeter £15 a year. So that he had an income of £44 a year – 17s. a week, fully twice the wage of an agricultural labourer in those days. He must have seemed well enough to do to many of his Helpstone neighbours. But it was just enough to prevent him from being a peasant, or anything else. His four visits to London between 1820 and 1825 must have made a great hole in his income. And that was exasperatingly dribbled out to him. Still worse, £100 of his trust fund, nominally given by his publisher, was in fact taken from his half-share of the profits on his first, and only really successful volume, and he was kept in ignorance of this. Not till 1829 did Clare succeed in getting a statement of accounts from Taylor. Thus for eight most important years Clare can have had no notion of what his financial position really was – and it turned out to be worse than his worst forebodings. He, who needed a new sense of responsibility, was treated like a child. When, finally, having fully realized the decline of his popularity, he made the sensible decision to set up as a smallholder at Northborough, he found he could not touch his capital even to stock his holding. It was no wonder that under such treatment he got steadily into debt. The amount of his indebtedness was trival. He seems to have overspent himself by about £5 a year – but that was quite enough to put a man of Clare's origins and habits in a condition of perpetual anxiety.

Clare suffered lamentably from a sense of insecurity. He sought escape from it in occasional drinking bouts, in affairs with women which afterwards racked his conscience; but much more significantly he escaped into an idealization of his own free childhood. Freedom became his most precious conception; and it seemed to him that, as a child, he had enjoyed it. In one sense, he exaggerated. As a little boy he had to work hard and long, though his parents did their utmost to spare him, and to give him what little education they could afford. But his early years were passed in the days before enclosure, when work in the open-field and the common of meadow and waste had much more interruption and variety, and his love of wild nature could find satisfaction at most moments of his daily task, except with his flail in the threshing-barn. For the grown-up villager, too, even if he was only a cottager, as Clare's father was, there was far more security under the old system – innumerable odds and ends to be picked up, of right and without trespass, to eke out their poverty – and this sense of a wide, though ragged, margin between his parents and pauperdom was part of the atmosphere Clare breathed as a boy. Thus there was solid substance to his feeling that the shades of the prison-house had closed upon him – a prison-house without security. This feeling, which he shared with the disinherited villagers, was immensely heightened in him by the fervour of his response to wild nature.

He felt he was caught in the toils. By the time he moved from Helpstone to Northborough, he was evidently in a highly nervous condition. On the face of it it seems excessive to regard a move of three miles as a journey into a strange and distant and hostile land. But by now Clare was clinging desperately to the security of the past. His native Helpstone, even though metamorphosed by enclosure, was home, familiar and safe. The beautiful poem, *The Flitting*, which he wrote on his removal, shows him conscious of what the unimaginative would call his weakness.

I dwell on trifles like a child,
  I feel as ill becomes a man,
And still my thoughts like weedlings wild
  Grow up and blossom where they can.
They turn to places known so long
  I feel that joy was dwelling there,
So home-fed pleasures fill the song
  That has no present joys to heir.

His thoughts 'grow up to blossom where they can', and they
could blossom only in the ambience of his memories of the
past. The description of his condition is simple, moving and
exact. The secret of his malaise and his instinctive mode of
escape from it is contained in another two lines of the same
poem.

  Strange scenes mere shadows are to me,
    Vague *impersonifying* things.

The mere otherness of Northborough tended to deprive
him of the sense of his own identity, for this was bound up
and consubstantial with the familiar places and faces of his
home 'town'. The experience or 'not feeling oneself' in strange
surroundings is common enough among ordinary people; it
was infinitely intensified in one whose emotional life had
flowed out into the minute particulars of his immediate
neighbourhood as Clare's had done for nearly forty years.
Very likely, the actual exile to Northborough, which in
prospect had meant the beginning of a new and independent
life to him, finally tipped the delicate balance of his mental
integrity. His identity was lost, only to be fitfully regained.
But the process took five years. During them he wrote much
of his loveliest nature-poetry.

Clare Revisited

§

The transfiguration of Mary Joyce into the genius of the paradisal past had begun long before he left Helpstone; but it proceeded apace at Northborough. Naturally, as the locus of his identity was increasingly transferred to the past, she became the guardian of his precious and precarious freedom of mind. In this transformation she lost her own particularity. More than once in his poems he confesses that he does not remember her face. Clare's biographers, Mr. and Mrs. Tibble, quote an entry in one of his notebooks, soon after he came to Northborough, in which he tells of a dream.

That Guardian spirit in the shape of a soul-stirring beauty again appeared to me with the very same countenance in which she appeared many years ago and in which she has since appeared at intervals and moved my ideas into ecstasy.

He gives particulars of his former dreams. In one, dreamed before any of his poems were published, she had guided him out of a vast crowd, in which he was insignificant and alarmed, into a bookshop where he saw three volumes lettered with his name; in a second, she had stood at his side in the Judgment and brought him the assurance that all was well. In the third, at Northborough, she seems merely to have reassured him by her presence.

These dreams of a beautiful presence, a woman deity, gave the sublimest conceptions of beauty to my imagination; and being last night with the same presence, the lady divinity left such a vivid picture of her visits in my sleep, dreaming of dreams, that I could no longer doubt her existence. So I wrote them down to prolong the happiness of my faith in believing her my guardian genius.

A romanticized, or De Quinceyized, version of the second of these dreams is given in *The Nightmare*, written between 1821 and 1824. In that poem the angelic figure is just identified with Mary, not by appearance but by voice. The identification seems to be carried on in two sonnets to Mary written at the same period. He does not know whether 'to blame or bless the fate' that parted them.

> Thou seem'dst an angel when I met thee first,
> Nor has aught made thee otherwise to me:
> Possession had not cloyed my love, nor curst
> Fancy's wild visions with reality.
> Thou art an angel still . . .

But the dream figure did not look like the actual Mary Joyce; and it is notable that the following verse, separating Mary's beauty from her actual self, occurs in perhaps the only pre-asylum poem in which Clare faces realistically the probability that the actual Mary had become completely indifferent to, and even scornful of him.

> Thy face was so familiar grown
>   Thyself so often nigh,
> A moment's memory, when alone
>   Would bring thee to mine eye;
> But now my very dreams forget
>   That witching look to trace;
> And though thy beauty lingers yet
>   It wears a stranger's face.

There seems, in fact, to have been a gulf between the Mary of his waking visions, whom he could picture clearly, as he did in the very beautiful *Daydream in Summer* and in *The Progress of Rhyme*, and the angelic figure of his dreams of sleep, who from his description was not in the least like the Mary of real life. How far the gulf was bridged between them it is hard to say. Perhaps a point of fusion is indicated in the lovely lyric written at Northborough.

> I loved thee, though I told thee not,
>   Right earlily and long,
> Thou wert my joy in every spot,
>   My theme in every song.
>
> And when I saw a strange face
>   Where beauty held the claim,
> I gave it like a secret grace,
>   The being of thy name.

There 'Mary' has become the word of power to distinguish beauty in woman – as it were, the seal of recognition. That would unite the two. The other link between them is the voice. As he woke from his second dream, according to *The Nightmare*:

> 'Twas Mary's voice that hung in her farewell;
> The sound that moment in my memory fell
> A sound that held the music of the past.

It is curious, and perhaps significant, that in two of his last poems written at Northborough, written more than twelve years after this, he seems to expand its meaning.

In *Love and Solitude* he prays for absolute solitude, hidden from

> the very noise of troublous man
> Who did and does me all the harm he can . . .
> Farewell to poesy – and leave the will;
> Take all the world away – and leave me still
> The mirth and music of a woman's voice
> That bids the heart be happy and rejoice.

Plainly, that is no longer the voice of a mortal woman, for he prays to be absolutely alone. It is the voice which 'holds the music of the past'. And *The Shy Lover*, written apparently at the same time, ends with the lines, addressed to the Mary of actual memory:

> The mind on thee and beauty's music dwells
> And listens to the sound of Glinton bells.

Glinton was Mary's home. Her voice, the sound of Glinton bells, and beauty's music have melted into one another, and they are the same as 'the music of the past'.

That, as far as one can decipher the record of incipient insanity, is the more precious conception of Mary which Clare cherished when he was taken from Northborough to the mental home at Epping. 'Mary' is the name for the principle of beauty in all things, and Mary's voice – whether actually remembered or merely imagined – is the music of beauty, and of the paradisal past in which beauty was perfect. She is also the guardian angel who has the keeping of Clare's identity. But a different kind of Mary has also emerged. This was the Mary whom he had become persuaded he had married, and by whom he had children. She does not appear in his poetry previous to his complete breakdown. Perhaps she was the product of a sort of precipitation of the potential ambivalence of the actual Mary, who had, in brutal fact, turned away from him. As she was, in one image, etherealized beyond recognition, so in the other, she was brought down to earth. And both these Marys appear together in the incoherences of *Don Juan* and *Child Harold*, which he wrote just before and after his escape from Epping in 1841. Perhaps it was inevitable that they should: for the motive of his escape seems to have been the desire to return in the body of this flesh into the paradisal past, and the conviction that he could do so. He believed he was going to meet the Mary who was his wife, and that his three years at Epping had been an enforced separation from her. The news that she was dead he regarded with part of his mind as a conspiratorial deception. With another part he recognized the truth – at least in the form that Mary was parted from him for ever. On the day of his arrival he wrote the pathetic poem which ends

> No ray of hope my fate beguiles
> I've lost love, home, and Mary.

Nevertheless it was for her that he wrote the account of his grim journey from Epping to Northborough, and as soon as he had finished it he added a letter to her, as to his wife.

Not being able to see you or to hear where you were I soon began to feel homeless at home and shall by and by feel nearly hopeless, but not so lonely as I did in Essex. For here I can see Glinton Church, and feeling that Mary is safe, if not happy, I am gratified. Though my home is no home to me, my hopes are not entirely hopeless while even the memory of Mary lives so near me.

To Dr. Allen he wrote, a little later:

One of my fancies I found here with her family and all well. . . . Where my poetical fancy is I cannot say, for the people in the neighbourhood tell me that the one called Mary has been dead these eight years. . . .

I care nothing about the women now, for they are faithless and deceitful. . . . Man I never did like – and woman has long sickened me. I should like to be to myself a few years and live the life of a hermit; but even there I should wish for her whom I am always thinking of – and almost every song I write has some sighs and wishes in ink about Mary.

What he told Dr. Allen of his songs is true. Much the most valuable of his poetry at this time is four pathetic songs about Mary, whom he believes to be at Glinton: mysteriously but inexorably kept from him. But in the letter to Allen is the prose truth of that ambivalence of Mary which so disturbs the poem *Child Harold*, to which he was still adding verses at this time. Something of it is carried over into the new dimension of his visionary poems three years later. Perhaps had he then attempted to write a long consecutive poem it would have been equally disturbing. But in the momentary inspiration of separate poems it was magically purified. As it were with the cessation of hope of an earthly meeting with his love, the painful and intolerable discords of *Don Juan* and *Child Harold* cease. The effect is as though, in the freedom he momentarily shared with God, he understood with God's understanding that Mary the faithless and Mary the faithful were one.

II

The Act of Parliament for enclosing Clare's native parish of Helpstone was passed in 1809, when Clare was sixteen. It must have taken another two or three years for the Commissioners to get their work done, and for the effects of the award to be visible. Within that time Clare's tongue-tied sweethearting with Mary Joyce came to a final end. Perhaps there was a connection. The award made Mary's father's holding of 75 acres in the open-field a compact little farm: more dignified and more profitable than before. Mary's father went further up in the world, Clare's went further down. There was distance enough between the families before – between a 75 acre man and a landless cottager like the illegitimate Parker Clare: now it was a gulf. John Clare was definitely far beneath Mary Joyce, and they parted. The loss of the freedom of the open-fields by enclosure and the loss of Mary may have been in fact, and not merely in Clare's creative imagination, a single happening.

In Clare's poetry, as nowhere else in our literature, we can see and feel the transformation of the countryside and the disruption of the old village community which was involved in that great and pitiless social revolution of which the Hammonds wrote the history. There were three main aspects of this radical change for the villager: loss of the open-fields and common meadow-land, loss of the commons and wastes, and loss of the margin that gave the feeling of independence. The first of these did not directly affect a man like Clare's father.

He owned no strip in the open-field and had no right of pasture in the meadows or on the stubbles. Those who did own a strip, or a few, or many, received an equivalent area under the award; but though in theory the smallest holders were no worse off, in practice they were. They had to fence their new holdings, and without the common they could no longer keep a cow. Clare's father, of course, never had kept one.

With the directly economic effects of the enclosure of the open-fields themselves Clare was not much concerned. They were outside his family horizon. But he gives a precious picture of the relative freedom of work in the open-field for boys of his kind in *The Lamentations of Round Oak Waters*. The stream speaks to him and reminds him how, when he was leading the horses or driving the plough-team (as a boy day-labourer), he used to think of it with longing.

> But now, alas! my charms are done
>   For Shepherds and for thee:
> The cowboy with his green is gone
>   And every bush and tree.
> Dire nakedness o'er all prevails;
>   You fallows, bare and brown,
> Are all beset with post and rails
>   And turned upside down.

So much for the common where Round Oak Waters ran. Now for the open-field itself.

> The gently curving darksome balks
>   That stript[1] the cornfields o'er

---

[1] 'Stript.' Does this mean 'striped' – showing like stripes, or 'stripped' – making strips of the open-field? Perhaps both at once.

And proved the shepherd's daily walks
    Now prove his walks no more.
The plough has had them under hand
    And overturned them all.
And now along the elting land
    Poor swains are forced to maul.

There are no more grassy balks for them to walk over; they must push their way over the soft new ploughed land.

And where yon furlong meets the lawn
    To ploughmen, ah! how sweet,
When they had their long furrow drawn,
    Its eddings to their feet,
To rest them while they cleaned their plough
    And light the loaded shoe –
But ah! there's ne'er an edding now
    For either me or you.

Eddings means headlands, and is presumably a dialect corruption of 'headings'; and the furlong is the standard strip in the open-field. Without Clare's picture, it would hardly occur to us how much the open-field relieved the monotony of labour – relieved it, of course, at the price of what the economists and the improvers called waste – of time and labour. But monotony does not make for happiness.

The balks and eddings are no more
    The pastures too are gone,
The greens, the meadows, and the moors
    Are all cut up and done.

Unprofessional Essays

There's scarce a greensward spot remains
  And scarce a single tree;
All naked are thy native plains,
  And yet they're dear to thee.

But it was above all the loss of the old commons and wastes – the 'greens' of which the old name persists even in the most unlikely places[1] – which most deeply affected Clare. The enclosing and ploughing up of these meant that the milkmaids from the 'town' – Clare almost always kept the Saxon name for the village and the village-community – no longer made their journeys by or through the open-field to and from their cows, carrying a 'gait' – two buckets on a yoke, and crying, 'Come, mull!' to their beasts,
There is a picture of one of them in *The River Gwash*.

The swinging milkmaid journeying from the town
  Skips o'er the stones that stride the meadow slough
And on thy banks she sets her bucket down
  To reach a wild rose ere she calls her cow.

But the green is under the plough.

Both milkmaid's shouts and herdsman's call
  Have vanish'd with the green,
The kingcups yellow, shades and all
  Shall nevermore be seen;

[1] My own horizon, as a child living in a densely populated suburb of South London, was bounded by two greens: Camberwell Green to the north and Goose Green to the south. On Goose Green one May Day I saw, and was frightened by, a mysterious column of green leaves slowly circling round on a pair of feet: an authentic Jack i' the Green. This was about 1896. It may have been the last in London.

But the thick-cultured tribes that grow
  Will so efface the scene,
That aftertimes will hardly know
  It ever was a green.

The 'thick-cultured tribes' are those heavy corncrops, profiting by the stored up fertility of the ancient grassland, which, understandably enough, rejoiced the heart of the improver, and widened the gulf between the farmer and the cottager. Indeed, they spelt the end of

The old freedom that was living then
When masters made them merry with their men,
And all their coats alike were russet brown
And his rude speech was vulgar as their own.

But the conversion into arable is not yet complete: the new crops have not yet quite effaced the old scene. Another glimpse of this moment of transition shows the green still resisting.

Yon flaggy tufts, and many a rushy knot
Existing still in spite of spade and plough,
As seeming fond and loath to leave the spot
Tell where was once the green – brown fallows now,
Where Lubin often turns a saddened brow,
Marks the stopt brook and mourns oppression's power
And thinks how once he waded in each slough
To crop the yellow 'horse-blob's' early flower.

The farmer in me, even now, cannot but rejoice a little over the disappearance of that slough and its marsh marigolds, when the brook – not really stopped, as Clare says, but controlled from wandering by a substantial drain-pipe – was prevented from turning a goodly patch of ground into a quagmire. The only reason why this could not be done without enclosure of the common was that everybody's business was, as ever, nobody's business. Enclosure had to come, if the land of England was to be lifted from agricultural stagnation. The evil was that it was done with such ruthlessness towards the poor villagers' precious and prescriptive rights. But even if even-handed justice had been done, Clare would not have liked the change any better than he did. What justice to the villager required was that in return for the loss of his rights, he should have had an acre or two of land to cultivate for himself. But the ensuing landscape – what would have met the eye – would have been much the same as the landscape which hurt Clare's heart.

In *Enclosure*, he tells first of what had been.

> Far spread the moory ground, a level scene,
> Bespread with rush and one eternal green . . .
> Cows went and came with every morn and night
> To the wild pasture as their common right;
> And sheep, unfolded with the rising sun,
> Heard the swains shout and felt their freedom won,
> Tracked the red fallow field and heath and plain,
> Or sought the brook to drink and roamed again.

The 'red fallow-field' was that part of the open-field, generally one-third, which was left a bare fallow for the year.

> Moors losing from the sight, far, smooth and blea,
> Where swept the plover in its pleasure free,

Are vanished now with heaths once wild and gay
As poet's visions of life's early day.
Like mighty giants of their limbs bereft
The sky-bound wastes in mingled garbs are left,
Fence meeting fence in owners' little grounds
Of field and meadow, large as garden grounds,
In little parcels little minds to please
With men and flocks imprisoned, ill at ease.

That, only with the little parcels still more plentiful, would have been the scene if justice had been done. In fact, the dispossessed villagers had little minds, in Clare's sense; they would have been vastly pleased with such little parcels if only they had received them. And Clare was always, very obviously, in two minds about the villager. At one moment he declares him unspoiled, at another a vulgar clown; at one moment he declares that he delights in the beauties of nature, at another that he is completely insensitive to them.

§

It would be false to imply that Clare's passionate preference for the old order was primarily aesthetic; but it is fair to emphasize that he was not primarily concerned with the social injustice of enclosure. What he loved about the old order was its freedom, in his own peculiar and characteristic sense of the word, in which freedom for the land itself bulked just as large as freedom for those who lived on and by the land. By idiosyncrasy he was deeply enamoured of wild nature; the more of it that was left, the better, he felt. And the old order of the open-field left about as much of it as was possible if there was to be any agriculture at all. What exasperated the champion of productive agriculture, delighted Clare. Sometimes he comes very near to saying – and even nearer to feeling – that it was better that the land should be wild and free than enclosed and productive. His poem on *Cowper Green* rather gives him away.

> Though no yellow plains allow
> Food on thee for sheep or cow
> Where on list'ning ears so sweet
> Fall the mellow low and bleat
> Greeting, on eve's dewy gale,
> Resting-fold and milking-pail;
> Though not these adorn thy scene,
> Still I love thee, Cowper Green . . .
>
> . . . Thy unmolested grass,
> Untouch'd even by the ass
> Spindled up its destined height,
> Far too sour for sheep to bite.

The first eight lines are unexceptionable. He loves it in spite of its poverty. But the epithets 'unmolested' and 'destined' in the concluding lines suggest that he preferred it poor: for then it was undisturbed. His intense sympathy with wild nature ended in a projection of his own passion for freedom on to the land. Hence the peculiar felicity he achieves in such a poem as *The Lament of Swordy Well*, where he makes the piece of waste speak for itself.

> I'm Swordy Well, a piece of land
>   That's fell upon the town,
> Who worked me till I couldn't stand
>   And crush me now I'm down . . .

Clare Revisited

> ... Vile enclosure came and made
> A parish slave of me.

Evidently, Swordy Well was left as a piece of waste for the
parish under the enclosure award. And the villagers were, to
Clare's sense, ruthless masters of it. They cultivated it while
the price of corn was high.

> When gain got high the tasteless tykes
> Grubbed up trees, banks and rushes ...

The 'tasteless tykes' must have been the villagers themselves.
Now, they have abandoned it again: they dig it only for 'sand
and grit and stones'.

> And should the price of grain get high
> – Lord help and keep it low! –
> I shan't possess a butterfly
> Nor get a weed to grow.
>
> I shan't possess a yard of ground
> To bid a mouse to thrive;
> For gain has put me in a pound,
> I scarce can keep alive.
>
> Ah me! they turned me inside out
> For sand and grit and stones,
> And turned my old green hills about
> And picked my very bones.

Clare so captures our sympathy for Swordy Well that we
almost forget that the villagers were only making the best use

they could of what seems to have been the only piece of waste remaining to them: indeed, the only piece in the parish 'save his Lordship's woods' that remained waste after enclosure.

Certainly, Clare loved the old open-field system most of all because it was the next best thing to leaving nature all wild. There was a stubborn core of the pure gipsy and vagabond in him. On his heart was written: The more freedom for Nature, the more freedom for me. And it is the gipsy or the poet, rather than the peasant, who laments in *The Village Minstrel* that, as everywhere under enclosure, the old meandering high-roads, with their wide grass verges remaining from the days when every waggon in wintertime had to make a fresh track to find solid ground, were reduced to a uniform width.

The thorns are gone, the woodlark's song is hush,
Spring now resembles winter more than spring,

(because the grass common is under the plough, with the grass balks of the open-field).

The shades are banish'd all – the birds have took to wing.
There once were lanes in nature's freedom dropt,
There once were paths that every valley wound –
Inclosure came and every path was stopt;
Each tyrant fixed his sign where paths were found
To hint a trespass now who crossed the ground:
Justice is made to speak as they command
The high road now must be each stinted bound:
– Inclosure thou'rt a curse upon the land,
And tasteless was the wretch who thy existence planned.

'Tasteless', again, like the tykes, not 'ruthless'. Not that the judgment can fairly be called aesthetic. In Clare's mind there are two criteria: beauty and freedom, and those, for him, were practically indistinguishable. Moreover, as we have seen, freedom for him is a birthright which belongs no less to nature than to man. Such a conception or ideal is purely romantic. The two freedoms could be reconciled only in a nomad society. Clare had not thought it out, and probably he had a resistance to doing so. And in regard to the specific problem of enclosure, there is no indication anywhere in his writings that he had formed any idea of what ought to have been done.

In actual practice, he chose to be a small-holder; but that, he might have said, was only when enclosure had become an accomplished fact. It was the best available in the new and alien world.

§

Clare, in short, never admitted to his own mind that enclosure was necessary at all. That the land ought to be made more productive was an alien thought which he never entertained. The one imperative was that the double freedom possible under the old order, and possible only under that order, should be retained. To change the order was to diminish the freedom: therefore it was oppression.

Oppression, in fact, there was: oppression such as broke the spirit of the agricultural worker for generations. But Clare never distinguished between the oppression of the villager, which was unnecessary and unjust, and the oppression of the land itself which was necessary – and, if the word has meaning, just. Behind Clare's copious and beautiful writing on the changing order lies one comprehensive and all-pervading metaphor akin to the pathetic fallacy: that by enclosure the land and the villagers are both imprisoned, and both groan under the new bondage. So, Swordy Well can speak as 'a parish-slave'; so, in *The Village Minstrel*, Clare can pass from one kind of oppression to the other as though they were essentially the same.

> O England! boasted land of liberty,
> With strangers still thou mayst thy title own,
> But thy poor slaves the alteration see,
> With many a loss to them the truth is known:
> Like emigrating birds thy freedom's flown,
> While mongrel clowns, low as their rooting plough,
> Disdain thy laws to put in force their own;
> And every village owns its tyrants now,
> And parish-slaves must live as parish kings allow.

It is by no means certain, even there, that the parish-slaves are human only. A little further, and they certainly are not.

> The haunts of freedom, cowherd's wattled bower
> And shepherds' huts, and trees that towered high
> And spreading thorns that turned a summer shower,
> All captives lost and past to sad oppression's power.

Gone were the town cowherd's and the town shepherd's desultory and delightful occupations, when they had leisure to sing their songs and tell their tales to the listening boy.

> O samely naked leas, so bleak, so strange!
> The rush-tuft gone that hid the skylark's nest.
> Ah, when will May morn hear such strains again?
> The storms beat chilly on its naked breast,
> No shelter grows to shield, no home invites to rest.

Countrymen of this generation had much the same feeling, when a piece of old daisy-pied grass came under the plough during the war years. How Clare would have shuddered at ley-farming and the modern maxim: Take the plough *all* round the farm!

Not merely in spite of, but because of enclosure, the land of England was to achieve a new rich beauty, which was to be threatened in its turn with destruction. Those same quick hedges which were being planted under Clare's eyes to divide the new fields came into their full glory, from his point of view, only when agriculture was again declining and farmers could no longer afford to pay men to trim and pleach them. Clare would have loved them as they were between the two wars – miniature copses six yards thick encroaching steadily on the fields. The eyesore to the farmer is a thing of beauty to the poet. But in truth agriculture itself, from Clare's point of view, is tyranny and oppression over wild nature; a violation, as he says in *Emmonsale Heath*:

> Stern industry with stubborn toil
>   And wants unsatisfied,
> Still leaves untouched thy maiden soil
>   In its unsullied pride.

What Clare gives us is a wonderful *picture* of enclosure. Through his percipient eye we see the landscape in the process and detail of change. We see the pathetic figures of the villagers who suffer as their little margin of subsistence is torn from them. We see, in *The Cress Gatherer*, the old widow whose husband had been the parish clerk, and who gathers the wisps of wool from the bushes from which she spins mops to sell for sixpence; she must have found her supply dwindle dreadfully when there were no more sheep on the thorny green. There is the village fortune-teller, the wife of the town herdsman.

> When her spouse
> Walked without sticks, he kept the village cows,
> Ere vile enclosure took away the moor
> And farmers built a workhouse for the poor.

There is the mole-catcher who also gathers cresses, and gathers leeches too, hunts for peewit's eggs, prods for eels, and with the shepherd's connivance steals a farmer's turnip for his breakfast. His meagre livelihood must have suffered when there was no more freedom to roam.

> When labour fails, the workhouse fare is near;
> And thus on misery's edge he potters round the year.

The workhouse is the grim and dreadful innovation. It is to be distinguished from the parish cottage – to which, as far as I remember, Clare never gives its traditional name of the 'town-house'. That was the old home for the village indigents – a free roof under which they received their pittance of out-relief and retained a degree of independence. The workhouse is a new building, which Clare definitely associates with enclosure and the new cleavage between the farmer and the labourer. Here the pauper was fed and clothed after a fashion and hired out to a farmer, if he was capable of work, his wages being paid to the overseer. He was, in fact, a slave.

Clare describes the new building in *The Parish*.

> Shoved as a nuisance from pride's scornful sight
> In a cold corner stands in woeful plight

Clare Revisited

The shuttered workhouse of the parish poor,
And towards the north wind opes its creaking door.
A makeshift shed for misery, no thought
Urged plans for comfort when the work was wrought,
No garden spot was left dull want to cheer
And make the calls of hunger less severe
With wholesome herbs that summer might supply;
'Twas not contrived for want to live, but die.
A forced concern to satisfy the law
Built want this covering o'er his bed of straw.
E'en that cheap blessing that's so freely given
To all that live beneath the face of heaven,
The light of day, is not allowed to win
A smiling passage to the glooms within;
No window opens on the southern sky –
A luxury deem'd to pride's disdainful eye.

The necessity for this grudging structure arose from the abolition of the marginal freedom which enabled the poor to eke out their parish relief. In the gulf between the town-house and the workhouse was swallowed the precious independence of those who lived on the edge of destitution.

One other consequence of enclosure is felt in Clare's poetry – the new fear of trespass. It appears in his *Narrative Verses*, describing a walk from Helpstone to Burghley. He had dallied so often in contemplation on the way that he was in danger of being overtaken by the dark: inward voices warned him.

I instantly obey'd their call,
     Nor went to where the footpath lay,
But clamber'd o'er an old rough wall
     And stole across the nearest way.

No spire I caught, nor woody swell,
  My eye confin'd to lower bounds,
Yet not to mark the flow'ret's bell,
  But watch the owners of the grounds;
Their presence was my only fear,
  No boughs to shield me if they came,
And soon amid my rash career
  I deem'd such trespassing to blame.

For troubled thoughts began to rise,
  Of ills almost beyond relief
Which might from this one cause arise,
  And leave me then to want reprief;
So arguing with myself how vain
  An afterthought 'still to keep free',
Made me to seek the road again,
  And own the force of liberty.

The penalties for trespass, and the danger of committing it, were vastly increased by enclosure. In a much later poem, the sonnet entitled *Trespass*, he gives a subtler account of the experience.

I dreaded walking where there was no path
And prest with cautious tread the meadow swath,
And always turned to look with wary eye,
And always feared the farmer coming by;
Yet everything about where I had gone
Appeared so beautiful I ventured on;
And when I gained the road where all are free,
I fancied every stranger frowned at me,

And every kinder look appeared to say,
'You've been on trespass in your walk today.'
I've often thought, the day appeared so fine,
How beautiful if such a place were mine;
But having naught, I never feel alone
And cannot use another's as my own.

There is expressed the most personal part of the tragedy of
enclosure for Clare. Because of it, the possibility of his precious
solitude now depends on private possession; and he, by nature
even more than by lack of wealth, was never interested in
possession. In the former days, he could possess nothing, and
yet be rich in solitude.

§

In the last analysis, I think, freedom – the experience, the
idea and the ideal which meant most to Clare all his life – was
for him the freedom to be alone with wild nature. That was a
conception of freedom which very few, if any, villagers shared
with him: it was eccentric to their concerns, beyond their
horizon. Thus it was rather by accident than essence, that Clare
so often appears to be the champion of the disrupted village-
community. True, he, by necessity, had been forced to work in
the fields and in the threshing barn at a tender age, and he knew
how much more enjoyable was the frequently interrupted
work in the open-field than the monotony of the flail. In so
far as under enclosure the work of the farm-labourer tended to
become more monotonous, his championship of the old order
was a championship of freedom for the individual villager.
But he had no real sympathy with the instinctive desire of the
peasants to become small property-owners as they did in

France. A villager is capable and eager for very 'stern industry' indeed, if he thereby improves his own position and not some-body else's. That prospect would have had no attractions for Clare; and since it would have involved the partitioning of the commons among the villagers, Clare's sense of disaster would have been just the same. In truth, enclosure of any kind, whether just or unjust to the villager, was anathema to Clare. It was *enclosure* – imprisonment: both of himself and wild nature. And the old order was 'freedom' for them both. His mind clung to it with passionate and undying regret.

All that is to say, perhaps, no more than that Clare was born a romantic poet – and an exceptionally pure example of the kind: purer than Wordsworth, purer than Blake. He would never have been stirred, as they, by revolutionary enthusiasm. His social Elysium was in the immediate past. Neither had he anything of Keats's hard-won philosophy of change – his vision of 'creations and destroyings' as a process at the very heart of reality. Change terrified and bewildered Clare; it was part of that 'strife' which was the alien mode of existence in the adult world, and which dismayed him. The 'strife' made him sick at heart, and he came to believe, or at least to hope, that it was one of 'earth's delusions' which would pass away. It is indeed remarkable how seldom the violence and oppression of Nature herself comes within his field of vision as a nature-poet. He instinctively ignored it. Keats did not like it any more than Clare did; but he could not ignore it.

> But I saw too distinct into the core
> Of an eternal fierce destruction,
> And so from happiness I far was gone.

Clare Revisited

Still am I sick of it: and though today
I've gathered young spring-leaves and flowers gay
Of perwinkle and wild strawberry,
Still do I that most fierce destruction see,
The shark at savage prey – the hawk at pounce,
The gentle robin, like a pard or ounce,
Ravening a worm.

The vision never left Keats: he made it the theme both of the
first and second *Hyperions*. Clare's overwhelming impulse was
to turn away from it. So he idealized his childhood and the
world of pre-enclosure days as a realm of joy and love and
peace – a static perfection that had been swept away. And
since the coming of enclosure synchronized with his emergence
from childhood to manhood; from freedom to responsibility;
and, in his experience of woman, from Mary to Martha,
enclosure was less a social revolution than a personal and
spiritual cataclysm.

Oh, I never thought that joys would run away from boys,
Or that boys would change their minds and forsake such
        summer joys;
But alack, I never dreamed that the world had other toys
To petrify first feeling like the fable into stone,
Till I found the pleasure past and a winter come at last,
Then the fields were sudden bare and the sky got overcast,
And boyhood's pleasing haunts, like a blossom in the blast,
Was shrivelled to a withered weed and trampled down and
        done
Till vanished was the morning spring and set the summer sun,
And winter fought her battle strife and won.

By Langley Bush I roam, but the bush hath left its hill,
On Cowper Green I stray, 'tis a desert strange and chill,
And the spreading Lea Close Oak, ere decay had penned its
  will,
To the axe of the spoiler and self-interest fell a prey,
And Crossberry Way and old Round Oak's narrow lane
With its hollow trees like pulpits I shall never see again.
Enclosure like a Buonaparte let not a thing remain,
It levelled every bush and tree and levelled every hill
And hung the moles for traitors – though the brook is running
  still,
It runs a naked stream, cold and chill.

Oh, had I known as then joy had left the paths of men,
I had watched her night and day, be sure, and never slept agen,
And when she turned to go, oh, I'd caught her mantle then
And wooed her like a lover by my lonely side to stay;
Ay, knelt and worshipped on, as love in beauty's bower,
And clung upon her smiles as a bee upon a flower,
And gave her heart my posies, all cropt in a sunny hour,
As keepsakes and pledges all to never fade away;
But love never needed to treasure up the may,
So it went the common road to decay.

Clare's feeling, as always, is pure; and it wrings the heart.
But it wrings the heart as the wail of a child. It is the terrible
fact of change, the passing away of the present into the irre-
vocable past, that is the cause of his misery: not the injustice
of enclosure. Enclosure is much more a symbol and a name
for the evil that has befallen him, in being driven out of the
paradise of childhood into the darkened ways of manhood,

than it is a thing in itself. And it is substantially true that he remained a child. Not that he did not develop as a poet. He did: each of his volumes shows a substantial poetical advance on the one before. But it is an advance towards subtler and more delicate expression within a restricted range of technique and feeling. The freedom of the paradisal past of childhood, the freedom of communion with Nature – these are his abiding realities. The world of men and women – this is the prison of deception and delusion: from which he incessantly seeks escape, either into the solitude of wild nature, or poetry, or more often into both together. His early address to *Solitude*:

> And I love thy presence drear
> In such wildernesses, where
> Ne'er an axe was heard to sound
> Or a tree's fall gulsh'd the ground,
> Where (as if that spot could be)
> First footmark'd the ground by me,
> And is still, and wild, and gay,
> Left as at creation's day.

is born of the same longing as his more desperate cry, twenty years later:

> I long for scenes were man hath never trod,
>   A place where woman never smiled or wept.

And in between, how many times, in how many forms, had he not uttered this longing for solitude, or his rapture in attaining it, as in *The Robin's Nest*:

> In this old spot
> I feel that rapture which the world hath not,
> That joy like health which flushes in my face
> Amid the brambles of this ancient place,
> Shut out from all but that superior power
> That guards and glads and cheers me every hour,
> That wraps me like a mantle from the storm
> Of care, and bids the coldest hope be warm,
> That speaks in spots where all things silent be
> In words not heard but felt.

So he declared: 'Solitude and God are one to me.'

This solitude was, for Clare, scarcely distinguishable from the condition of poetry: for the making of poetry was, for him, an incessant insulation of his secret self from the strife of the world, a continual entry or re-entry into the realm of freedom and joy and love which had been his as a child: the true kingdom of God, in his simple theology. And this communion of solitude he was constantly establishing between himself and the dumb creatures of earth, in an instinctive intensity of contemplation and passion of sympathy which insulated them and him just as a pair of lovers are insulated in a crowded train in the Underground. Thus his intensely personal love of nature came to coalesce in his mind with the memory of his childhood affection for Mary Joyce, so that by a simple alchemy she became the symbol and guardian of his secret felicity – the goddess of his solitary communion, the muse of his poetry, the angel of his freedom, the still unravished bride of his quietness.

The purity of the love which comprehended all these things – nature, freedom, Mary – in a communion of the imagination was always unsullied in Clare, when he was himself: for what he felt to be his true self was homogeneous with it. It was immune from the world's slow stain. The time came when he could no longer hold on to it; when the gate to the realm of love and freedom was closed so that he could no longer enter it at will. Then he had lost his identity: he regained it, and the kingdom to which it was native, only at fitful intervals. But the purity was incorruptible.

Whitman: Poet-prophet of Democracy

Whitman: Poet-prophet of Democracy

*

IT is now nearly fifty years since my classical tutor at Oxford, H. F. Fox – whom I name, though his name will be meaningless to others, for the private satisfaction of commemorating him – pressed upon me Whitman's *Democratic Vistas*. Fox belonged to the old generation of English Liberals, who flourished in the latter decades of the nineteenth century. As a political force, they reached their apogee in the famous general election of 1906, when the Liberal party swept into power on a wave of universal reaction against the imperialist fervours of the South African war; and they were broken, permanently, by the First World War, which was undreamt of by their philosophy. But their fortunes as politicians are irrelevant. The best of the Liberals – such a one survives still in Gilbert Murray – were not politicians: they were idealists. And for one of them *Democratic Vistas* was a sort of modern Bible. I imagine that this was true of many others.

They were not mistaken in saluting Whitman as their prophet. *Democratic Vistas* is surely a permanent statement not only of the ideal of liberal democracy, but of its fundamental principles, which if it violates, it ceases to be. Democracy is a debased and ambiguous word today, when the spokesmen of totalitarian Russia make their monstrous claim that their society is a democracy, and have it granted even by some millions of Western Europeans. Therefore, I prefer to call the society which Whitman envisaged and championed, the free society. But the name is immaterial. There is no mistake possible about the kind of society of which Whitman was the prophet and champion.

> That which really balances and conserves the social and political world is not so much legislation, police, treaties, and dread of punishment, as the latent eternal intuitional sense, in humanity, of fairness, manliness, decorum, etc. Indeed, this perennial regulation, control, and oversight, by self-suppliance, is *sine qua non* to democracy; and a highest, widest aim of democratic literature may well be to bring forth, cultivate, brace and strengthen this sense, in individuals and society. A strong mastership of the general inferior self by the superior self, is to be aided, secured, indirectly, but surely, by the literatus, in his works, shaping for individual or aggregate democracy, a great passionate body, in and along with which goes a great masterful spirit.

That is, at once, a proclamation of Whitman's ideal of democracy, and of the part he felt that he was called to play in its realization. It is noble and compelling. And of *Democratic Vistas* in general it may be said that, apart from its own intrinsic merits, which are very great, it is necessary to an understanding of the real purpose of *Leaves of Grass*.

Yet this was the book of which Whitman wrote to Dowden in 1872 that 'it remains quite unread, uncalled for, here in America'. Though there is the best precedent for a prophet being without honour in his own country, in the case of Whitman it needs some explanation. The one which occurs most readily to an Englishman is that the Americans of Whitman's time were too engrossed in the material mastering of a continent to have time to pause and take their spiritual bearings, whereas the little body of contemporary and influential Englishmen, who received his work with enthusiasm, had, whether consciously or not, the premonition that the epoch of their country's expansion was over, and that if Britain was to retain significance as a power for civilization, it must be as a paradigm of the free society. Whitman made his impact upon Britain at a moment when its best minds were engaged in taking spiritual stock of their country. Carlyle, Ruskin, Arnold, and Morris were the influences which had worked on the younger men who were receptive to Whitman; and Whitman seemed to corroborate and combine those influences in a radically new way. He shifted the balance from the critical to the creative, from dubiety to faith; and he added a comprehensive assertion – a poetic demonstration – of the validity of the individual which came to his English disciples as a great liberation.

What Whitman was attempting in *Leaves of Grass* cannot be better described than in the words of *Democratic Vistas*:

> The literature, songs, esthetics, etc., of a country are of importance principally because they furnish the materials and suggestions of personality for the men and women of that country, and enforce them in a thousand effective ways.

Very likely, this purpose was not fully conscious in him when he began writing *Leaves of Grass*; indeed, he admitted it. But this is what he subsequently believed he had done, or tried to do. His belief was well-founded, and his claim just.

This we must allow, whether or not we share his belief that a national literature is principally of importance because it offers suggestions and materials for what he elsewhere calls 'a basic model or portrait of personality for general use'. Even those who hold that literature has other purposes to serve which seem to them more important, must allow that much of the world's great literature has been valued by the people for whom it was written for the concrete ideal of personal conduct it set before them. This was the merit of Homer in the eyes of a Greek, and of Virgil in the eyes of a Roman.

Such was the sense in which Whitman claimed to be the poet-prophet of America. There was nothing narrowly national in his conception of 'these States'. If at first sight it sometimes appears to be so, only a little patience and receptiveness is needed to make us realize that his insistence on the places, the persons, and the society with which he was familiar is only an example of the working of Goethe's poetical axiom that the universal is the particular. The universal of which 'these States' were the particular in Whitman's poetry is Democracy; and all over the world democrats, in Whitman's peculiar and profound sense of the word, that is, those who believe that a self-governing society of free and responsible individuals offers the only way of corporate progress towards the Good, have had no difficulty in regarding Whitman's America as the city of their own soul. It is for them a symbol of the ideal, of the same order as Blake's Albion and Jerusalem; and Whitman, in rhapsodizing over the rivers and prairies and people of America, is behaving as Shakespeare's poet, 'who gives to airy nothing a local habitation and a name' – except that the ideal democracy is much more than 'an airy nothing'.

Whitman: Poet-prophet of Democracy

It is at least a compelling vision of the society towards which humanity must stumble on, if it is not to cease to be human.

§

At the present moment many Western Europeans, who have an emotional and intellectual loyalty to the ideal of the free society, are tempted to be a little dubious towards America's claim to be its prototype. To them the activities of Senator McCarthy loom large and ominous. They should remember that Whitman himself passed through many periods of despondence in the days of the carpet-baggers and afterwards. He too cried: 'These savage, wolfish parties alarm me – owning no law but their own will, more and more combative, less and less tolerant of the idea of ensemble and of equal brotherhood, the perfect equality of the States, the ever overarching American ideas.' Nevertheless, Whitman held to his faith that these ugly and depressing manifestations were the grim growing pains inseparable from the process of the working out of a high destiny in a mass of common humanity. Whether his faith will be justified by the event, who can say? But there is scope for tempered optimism, when we remember that, in the years immediately following Whitman's death, another idealist, of a different kidney indeed, but equally combining with his idealism a robust realism, wrote of the condition of the United States.

Turn to Republican America. America has no Star Chamber, and no feudal barons. But it has Trusts; and it has millionaires whose factories, fenced in by live electric wires and defended by Pinkerton retainers with magazine rifles, would have made a Radical of Reginald

Front de Bœuf. Would Washington or Franklin have
lifted a finger in the cause of American independence if
they had foreseen its reality?

So wrote Bernard Shaw at the turn of the nineteenth century.
After fifty years those conditions seem to belong to a pre-
historic past, as do the conditions which produced the two
epoch-making strikes – of the dockers and the match-factory
girls – in England. Democracy is at least free to mend its
ways.

It is notable that Shaw, who no doubt imbibed much of his
doctrine from Whitman, or rather found in Whitman a
corroboration of his own native intuitions, agreed with him
whole-heartedly in his insistence on the importance of sexual
selection. The whole of *Man and Superman* might fairly be
regarded as Shaw's effort to put a sharper and more paradoxical edge on one of Whitman's central doctrines: the
necessity for Democracy of true and generous mating between
mentally, morally and physically developed men and women.
Indeed, Whitman not only anticipated Shaw's doctrine of the
necessity of the Superman for viable Democracy when he
inveighed against 'the appalling depletion of women in their
powers of sane athletic maternity' and proclaimed that the
radical weakness of the actual society in America was that
'the men believe not in the women, nor the women in the
men'; but in *Children of Adam* he was the palpable forerunner
of D. H. Lawrence's even more revolutionary teaching on sex.
Lawrence was directly indebted to Whitman even for much of
his distinctive phraseology.

This fructification in the soil of such different natures of
seeds scattered from Whitman's luxuriant flowering is a

simple and pertinent example of his immense seminal influence, as the poet-prophet of Democracy. That was what he justly claimed to be; and as such he is best comprehended. Or, at least, that is the best line of approach towards a complete understanding of his work: on one condition, that it is realized that Democracy can be justified and believed in only on the basis of a prior conviction of the infinite worth of the individual. Without this, Democracy is, what Plato held it to be, merely a short road to the tyranny of the baser elements in man. That can be avoided only by stubborn adherence to the sacrosanct principle of the divine right of the minority – of all minorities save one perhaps – to freedom of thought and speech. I call this right divine, because it cannot be rationally demonstrated. If it is self-evident, as I believe, it is self-evident only as a religious truth: ultimately, therefore, a matter of revelation. And since, even in the contemporary world, the truth has been categorically denied by the vast social organization of Russia, and since, in the ancient and mediaeval worlds, it was not admitted at all, it is evident that the apprehension of this religious truth is in constant need of renewal.

This was Whitman's great achievement. He vitally renewed the religious revelation on which the justification and continued existence of Democracy depends. That is to say, he experienced the revelation anew. From this derives the uniqueness of his work: the confidence with which he propounds the totality of himself – the whole experiencing nature which was Walt Whitman – as the citizen of the ideal Democracy. To the congenitally unsympathetic this has appeared as overweening arrogance, an awful example of the extravagance of romantic egotism. But no one responsive to Whitman has ever been repelled by this idiosyncrasy. It shocks only those to whom everything about Whitman is shocking. For in fact, his apparent egotism is entirely justified. It follows necessarily from his vision of the ideal society: for it is implicit in the ethos of that society that the individual shall be accepted with all his imperfections – warts and all. It is a society in which the individual person is valid, because it is a society whose law is love – the same society, in fact, of which the vision came to Tchehov when he listened to music: 'where everything is forgiven and it would be strange not to forgive.' In Christian idiom, it is the Kingdom of Heaven on earth. That may seem very remote from any practical Democracy we know or can foresee, either in America or Europe: but the imaginative vitality of the ideal is absolutely necessary to the continuing existence of any Democracy at all.

That is to say, behind and beneath Whitman's promulgation of his total self as a type of the citizen of the ideal Democracy is a deeply religious humility. Unless his 'egotism' is apprehended against this background of religion it is bound to be misunderstood. Not that there is any excuse for ignoring the background. Nothing could be more explicit than, for example, *Starting from Paumanok*.

Each is not for its own sake,
I say the whole earth and all the stars in the sky are for
      religion's sake.

I say no man has ever yet been half devout enough,
None has ever yet ador'd or worship'd half enough,
None has begun to think how divine he himself is, and how
      certain the future is.

I say that the real and permanent grandeur of these States
    must be their religion,
Otherwise there is no real and permanent grandeur;
(Nor character nor life worthy the name without religion,
Nor land nor man nor woman without religion.)

It may fairly be said that Whitman's great struggle as poet-prophet was to communicate his religious sense – of the divinity of the created world; of the democratic idea; of himself as part of the one and prophet of the other – without emasculating it by using the conventional language of religion. And that, in turn, is no small part of the problem for critical appreciation of him. What we are constrained to call Whitman's humility is not very like what is ordinarily understood by the word. It is the attitude of one who has been, once for all, possessed by the conviction that he is merely the vehicle and instrument of the One – 'the fang'd and glittering One whose head is over all'; who, at the same time and as part of the same experience, is convinced of the uniqueness of every created person, animal and thing; who, in the words of Meister Eckhart, is as one 'who having looked upon the sun, henceforward sees the sun in all things'.

To be possessed by this conviction is, inevitably, felt as an immense privilege, for with it descends, also inevitably, a sense of one's total validity – no greater, indeed, than that of any blade of grass or lily of the field, but since it happens to a human being with the burden of consciousness and self-consciousness, bringing with it an incomparable awareness of integration, of liberation, and of ordinariness. To a man who has passed through this experience, egotism and humility are indistinguishable. The completest self-utterance is not an assertion but an annihilation of the self. The ego which, according to Pascal, is 'always hateful', is by this experience transcended or abolished.

The proof of this, in Whitman's case, is easily available. No one who has responded to the personality exposed in *Leaves of Grass* has ever felt him to be other than lovable. One may be, indeed many are, completely allergic to him; but once he has found an entry, he takes possession: and that by a quite different process from conquering our aesthetic sensibilities. Not many of Whitman's poems overcome us by the perfection of their beauty; and in face of his achievement as a whole, we remain entirely aware of the crudeness, the imperfection, the failure in transmutation, of much of it. Nevertheless, we would not have it otherwise. The roughnesses, the blemishes belong. They are necessary to the kind of communication at which he aimed, and in which he believed. He well knew what he was doing when he insisted on the interdependent wholeness of the *Leaves* he had strung together. When he said 'the words of my book nothing, the drift of it everything', or more arrestingly, but not more profoundly, that 'he who touches this book, touches a man', he was saying the same thing: that he, as a whole, had been validated.

§

To get to the root of this conviction, in Whitman himself and those who respond to him, we should need to inquire into the nature of the mystical experience, when it happens to a man who has worked himself free of adherence to any particular system of religion. Such an inquiry would probably not be very rewarding. It is better to accept and ponder what Whitman himself has to say of it, in the *Song of Myself.*

I believe in you my soul, the other I am must not abase itself
    to you,
And you must not be abased to the other.

Loafe with me on the grass, loose the stop from your throat,
Not words, not music or rhyme I want, not custom or lecture,
    not even the best,
Only the lull I like, the hum of your valvèd voice.

I mind how once we lay such a transparent summer morning,
How you settled your head athwart my hips and gently
    turn'd over upon me,
And parted the shirt from my bosom-bone, and plunged your
    tongue to my bare-stript heart,
And reach'd till you felt my beard, and reach'd till you held
    my feet.

Swiftly arose and spread around me the peace and knowledge
    that pass all the argument of the earth.
And I know that the hand of God is the promise of my own,
And I know that the spirit of God is the brother of my own,
And that all the men ever born are also my brothers, and the
    women my sisters and lovers,
And that a kelson of the creation is love,
And limitless are leaves stiff or drooping in the fields,
And brown ants in the little wells beneath them,
And mossy scabs of the worm fence, heap'd stones, elder,
    mullein, and poke-weed.

That seems to be a description of an actual moment of illumination, perhaps *the* moment. By its curious and impressive particularity it recalls nothing so much as some equally particular and impressive passages in Blake's prophetic books. What is peculiar to Whitman is the intensity of his physical memory of the process (which other mystics have described) by which his corporeal body was, as it were, consumed and spiritualized. He describes it, vividly and memorably, as a physical caress of his body by his soul; and this swift and sudden transcending of the distinction and opposition between body and soul is accompanied by a vision of the infinite significance of the details of the created world – what Blake called the Minute Particulars – and a simultaneous assurance that 'a kelson of the creation is love'.

One may guess that this experience is the creative kernel of the whole of the *Song of Myself*: the seed of which that great poem is an exfoliation, though of course there is no way of proving it. Anyhow, it is certain that only in the perspective established by an experience such as he describes can the apparent contradictions of the poem be naturally resolved, and seen as necessary. If the experience is not the originating germ of the poem, it is the key to it. And at no point in the amazingly rich variety of its validations does Whitman go beyond what is warranted by his mystical assurance that everything everywhere is good and divinely appointed: himself, in all his thoughts, emotions and acts, no more and no less than any other particle of the universe. The self that he 'promulges' is the self that he has discovered at the point of its unity with the All; it is beneath anything that we are accustomed to regard as personality. He has been carried back to the ground of the personal (in the metaphysical sense of the word, ground) and has found it to be of one eternal substance with everything that is, or has been, or will be. This is the firm and timeless foundation from which he vaticinates.

Quite obviously, the *Song of Myself* is just as much, if not more preponderantly, the song of Whitman's not-Self, of all the richness of the objective world. Its 'egotism' is transparent and crystalline: it is completely acknowledged, and in no way apologized for –

> I know perfectly well my own egotism,
> Know my omnivorous lines and must not write any less,
> And would fetch you, whoever you are, flush with myself.

'Flush with myself' is one of those simple and superb phrases which Whitman always had at his command. It means not merely bringing his comrade-reader to the point where he shares Whitman's perception, but bringing them both together to coalesce in a common spiritual ether. He expresses this in a splendid and homely metaphor (which may not be recognized as a metaphor) at the beginning of his *Song*.

> Houses and rooms are full of perfumes, the shelves are crowded
>   with perfumes,
> I breathe the fragrance myself and know it and like it,
> The distillation would intoxicate me also, but I shall not let it.

> The atmosphere is not a perfume, it has no taste of the dis-
>   tillation, it is odorless,
> It is for my mouth forever, I am in love with it,
> I will go to the bank by the wood and become undisguised
>   and naked,
> I am mad for it to be in contact with me.

That is not, what it seems, a paean to the open air; it celebrates what Blake called 'the cleansing of the doors of perception', and the entry into the new and ever-present world of things as they are. Whitman calls 'the atmosphere' what Spinoza calls the *species aeternitatis*, and more traditionally Christian mystics the all-sustaining love of God. And so Whitman ends what is in deceptive appearance an invocation of the open air with a plain declaration of his real meaning.

Have you reckon'd a thousand acres much? Have you
    reckon'd the earth much?
Have you practis'd so long to learn to read?
Have you felt so proud to get at the meaning of poems?

Stop this day and night with me and you shall possess the
    origin of all poems,
You shall possess the good of the earth and sun (there are
    millions of suns left),
You shall no longer take things at second or third hand, nor
    look through the eyes of the dead, nor feed on the spectres
    in books,
You shall not look through my eyes either, nor take things
    from me,
You shall listen to all sides and filter them from yourself.

To be intoxicated by the perfume and the distillation which he loves, but puts aside for the pure serene of 'the atmosphere', is the same as looking through the eyes of the dead. It is not enough to call the condition at which he aims for himself, and which he seeks to induce in us, freshness of vision, though no doubt where that occurs a momentary transparence has taken place. He is urging us towards not a mere 'moment of vision' but to an understanding of all that it involves: towards making the religion that underlies all such moments a permanent possession. The *Song of Myself* is crowded to overflowing not only with moments of vision but also with a rich multiplicity of statements and explorations of the background from which it arises. His focus changes incessantly. At one moment, impersonal as 'the atmosphere', his 'omnivorous lines' roam over all America; at another they pass up and down the vistas of 'the Me myself', who no less belongs to all men.

The range of this great poem is wonderful: from the picture of the negro dray-driver:

The negro holds firmly the reins of his four horses, the block swags underneath on its tied-over chain,
The negro that drives the long dray of the stone-yard, steady and tall he stands pois'd on one leg on the string-piece,
His blue shirt exposes his ample neck and breast and loosens over his hip-band,
His glance is calm and commanding, he tosses the slouch of his hat away from his forehead,
The sun falls on his crispy hair and moustache, falls on the black of his polish'd and perfect limbs. –

to 'the mechanic's wife with her babe at her nipple interceding for every person born'. That sudden identification of the mechanic's wife with the Blessed Virgin is of the essence of Whitman's thought.

§

Thus the *Song of Myself*, rightly considered, is the explication of an eternal moment. If one is required to choose, this must be pronounced Whitman's greatest poem, and certainly the one around which all the other leaves of grass – the obviously beautiful and the apparently ungainly – naturally cluster themselves. It is the heart and core of the total pattern. The only poem I know with which it can be compared is Blake's *Milton*, which is also the explication of an eternal moment. There is one salient difference between them. Blake's wonderful poem is an exploration, or re-creation of the timeless instant, whereas Whitman's equally wonderful one is a declaration of its consequences. But *Milton* is barred from the common understanding by Blake's use of his esoteric symbols, where Whitman intently addressed himself, as far as he could, to the comprehension of the common man. But, for all that, the affinities between the two poems are astonishing. How perfectly, one feels, would such a passage as this from *Milton* fall into place in the *Song of Myself*!

Thou seest the Constellations in the deep and wondrous
  Night:
They rise in order and continue their immortal courses
Upon the mountains and in vales with harp and heavenly
  song,
With flute and clarion, with cups and measures fill'd with
  foaming wine.
Glitt'ring the streams reflect the Vision of beatitude,
And the calm Ocean joys beneath and smooths his awful waves.
These are the Sons of Los, and these the Labourers of the
  Vintage.
Thou seest the gorgeous clothed Flies that dance and sport in
  summer
Upon the sunny brooks and meadows: every one the dance

Knows in its intricate mazes of delight artful to weave:
Each one to sound his instruments of music in the dance,
To touch each other and recede, to cross and change and
    return:
These are the Children of Los; thou seest the Trees on moun-
    tains,
The wind blows heavy, loud they thunder thro' the darksome
    sky,
Uttering prophecies and speaking instructive words to the
    sons
Of men: These are the Sons of Los: These the Visions of
    Eternity,
But we see only as it were the hem of their garments
When with our vegetable eyes we view these wondrous
    Visions.

Save for the repeated phrase, 'These are the sons of Los',
which belongs to Blake's particular drama of the spirit, it
might well be one of Whitman's canticles. And when Whitman declares that he knows that

    limitless are leaves stiff and drooping in the fields
And brown ants in the little wells beneath them. –

he is saying precisely what Blake has said before him. The
leaves are 'limitless' because they are 'visions of eternity' and
we see only the hem of their garments.

Thus it was right and natural that Anne Gilchrist, who
devoted the first years of her widowhood to completing her
husband's *Life of William Blake*, the first book in which his
extraordinary genius was vindicated, should have been the

first woman publicly to salute the kindred genius of Whitman. By endorsing his radical utterances on sex (essentially the same as Blake's), she gave him perhaps the most precious support he ever received – 'the proudest word that ever came to me from a woman – if not the proudest word of all from any source', as he told Traubel.

Perhaps paradoxically, but rightly, Whitman believed that the immediate apprehension of an infinite significance in all existences was within the natural capacity of the common man. The truths he enunciated were self-evident to the natural vision: though he was constrained in honesty to admit that natural vision was not very common, since it required the removal of the scales of custom and prejudice – indeed of most of what was reckoned respectable.

> Long enough have you dream'd contemptible dreams,
> Now I wash the gum from your eyes.

Still, he insisted on the ordinariness of his own vision.

> Only what proves itself to every man and woman is so,
> Only what nobody denies is so.

Behind this simple asseveration is the justified assumption that, if Democracy is not a pretentious sham, a merely temporary form of social organization, produced by a favourable and quite exceptional conjunction of circumstances, and doomed to collapse under the pressure of any positive demands on its assumed morality, then there must be latent in its citizens a real fund of common and unshakable religious conviction. Every member, or at least the majority of its members, must be deeply persuaded of the infinite worth of others as well as himself. This axiomatic moral and religious truth may be overlaid, obscured and forgotten: but it must be there, or Democracy is an illusion. Whitman could not admit that it was, any more than I can. The most he could do was to admit the possibility that men might make the great refusal.

Once unquestioning obedience, once fully enslaved,
Once fully enslaved, no nation, state, city of this earth, ever
    afterward resumes its liberty.

But he had to make the act of faith in his fellows. The revelation that had come to consciousness in him, was latent in them. He was merely their spokesman, the interpreter of themselves to themselves.

I do not say these things for a dollar, or to fill up the time
    while I wait for a boat,
(It is you talking just as much as myself, I act as the tongue
    of you,
Tied in your mouth, in mine it begins to be loosen'd.)

And this is true, not merely of the great democratic common-places to which they might be expected to respond, but of the comprehensive religious realization on which alone the commonplaces can be grounded.

The moth and the fish eggs are in their place,
The bright suns I see and the dark suns I cannot see are in
    their place,
The palpable is in its place and the impalpable is in its place.

These are really the thoughts of all men in all ages and lands,
    they are not original with me,
If they are not yours as much as mine they are nothing, or next
    to nothing . . .

It is indeed the *philosophia perennis* which he proclaims, but
with the radical variation that he proclaims it to a society
which is, or claims to be, based on the belief that all its members
are at least capable of it. To them he says: Have the courage of
yourselves, first by discovering what your self really is. Get
down to the bedrock, the point at which you know your own
infinitude, stretching forward and backward in time, and
upwards to eternity. From that security go your way, fulfil
your own unique destiny.

I have no chair, no church, no philosophy,
I lead no man to a dinner-table, library, exchange,
But each man and each woman of you I lead upon a knoll,
My left hand hooking you around the waist,
My right hand pointing to landscapes of continents and the
    public road.

Not I, not anyone else can travel that road for you,
You must travel it for yourself.

It is not far, it is within reach,
Perhaps you have been on it since you were born and did not
    know,
Perhaps it is everywhere on water and on land.

Whitman: Poet-prophet of Democracy

§

Whitman's hope that ordinary men and women would straightway receive his utterances as the expression of their own deepest, but inarticulate, thoughts and feelings, was not realized in fact. He may have found a few such readers, but for the most part he had to depend on a few doughty defenders in his own country – Emerson supreme among them – and the enthusiastic support of a band of young English disciples. Indeed, writing so late as 1904, Henry Bryan Binns, his English biographer, speaking of Whitman's dismissal in 1865 from his clerkship in the Indian Office in Washington, as the result of the reading of *Leaves of Grass* by his Methodist chief, says: 'Average American opinion was then undisguisedly hostile, as, of course, it still remains.' If that was really the situation in America in 1904, it was distinctly different from that in England, where by that time his book had been accepted as a classic by the Liberal intellectuals, and as a sort of Bible by the native British Socialist movement, which, though it had a fair sprinkling of intellectuals, had a solid working-class core. Perhaps the explanation of this discrepancy is that quite early in the nineteenth century the British working class had become more or less completely urbanized, and Whitman's poetry had, for that part of it which was sufficiently alert to become Socialist, a powerful nostalgic attraction as a poetry of the open country and the open air. And it is very probable that the curious, but very marked association of the early Socialist movement in England with camping and hiking, on foot or cycle, in the countryside is almost entirely due to the influence of Whitman.

But that topic, though interesting, belongs to British local

history. It would appear, from what I have read, that it was
as a person rather than as a poet that Whitman came closest
to the common man in America: pre-eminently during his
hospital experiences in Washington in the Civil War, which
made so profound an impression upon him. It has been said
that Whitman attributed to his war-experiences a significance
for his literary development which they did not really possess.
This is true, in so far as the greater part of his most characteristic
work was written before the War. Nevertheless, Whitman
was not mistaken about himself. The war-experience did
deepen his understanding of his own poetic purposes; it
intensely sharpened his sense of the appalling cost even of the
partial realization of the democratic ideal; it summoned him
to make his own faith stronger in that which endures beyond
death. That involved no break in his development: no such
catastrophic change as, for example, was enforced upon the
consciousness of many Englishmen by their experiences of the
First World War. Whitman's faith was as deeply grounded
as any could be. There is at least one passage in the *Song of
Myself* in which he deliberately compares himself with the
crucified and resurrected Christ. It was a brave thing to do; but
in its splendid context it provokes no resistance.

Enough! enough! enough!
Somehow I have been stunn'd. Stand back!
Give me a little time beyond my cuff'd head, slumbers, dreams,
    gaping,
I discover myself on the verge of a usual mistake.

That I could forget the mockers and insults!
That I could forget the trickling tears and the blows of the
    bludgeons and hammers!

That I could look with a separate look on my own crucifixion
    and bloody crowning.

I remember now,
I resume the overstaid fraction,
The grave of rock multiplies what has been confided to it, or
    to any graves,
Corpses rise, gashes heal, fastenings roll from me.

I troop forth replenish'd with supreme power, one of an
    average unending procession,
Inland and sea-coast we go, and pass all boundary lines,
Our swift ordinances on their way over the whole earth,
The blossoms we wear in our hats the growth of thousands
    of years.

This, again, can be paralleled in the writings of Blake, for
whom the unity of all humanity is typified in 'the Divine
Humanity, the One Man, even Jesus', whose sufferings must
be renewed in the ascent of any single soul towards Eternity.
I recall Whitman's words here only to show that there was
already that in him which could endure his Civil War experiences without dismay, though receiving them with the full
sensitivity of the sympathetic and compassionate imagination.
He saw many Christs in the agonizing soldiers he tended.

It was wholly natural, therefore, that his participation in
their heroic sacrifice should deepen his conception of the
Democracy for which they died, and that he should declare:

Only the occurrence of the Secession War, and what it
show'd me as by flashes of lightning with the emotional

depths it sounded and arous'd . . . only from the strong
flare and provocations of that war's sights and scenes the
final reasons-for-being of an autochthonic and passionate
song finally came forth.

At any rate it seems to me that from this point onward,
Whitman understood his purpose more clearly as that of the
poet-prophet of a society to be actually realized, as it had
actually been paid for in limitless human suffering. He had
the satisfaction of knowing that he too had paid the price. The
immense demands of the hospital-years in Washington on his
vital energy were the cause of his paralysis, and of the relative
poverty of his subsequent poetic output.

To compensate, there is the admirable vaticination of
Democratic Vistas. The vision and argument of this book, more
directly than any of the poetry in *Leaves of Grass*, arise from
his war-experience. This, he seems to say, is the society of
which that manifest heroism of the common man offers the
earnest.

The movements of the late secession war, and their results,
to any sense that studies well and comprehends them,
show that popular democracy, whatever its faults and
dangers, practically justifies itself beyond the proudest
claims and wildest hopes of its enthusiasts.

We who have lived to see much the same common men
fight with no less heroism and endure no less suffering in
defence of a system so remote from democracy as the Com-
munism of Stalin's Russia or the National Socialism of
Hitler's Germany, may be more dubious of the validity of

this demonstration. But it seemed cogent to Whitman; and perhaps he was right. And there is no doubt at all that he was right in his vindication of the Democracy he envisioned as the only form of society which can claim the moral allegiance of the free man.

> The purpose of democracy . . . is, through many trans-migrations and amid endless ridicules, arguments, and ostensible failures, to illustrate, at all hazards, this doctrine or theory that man, properly trained in highest, sanest freedom, may and must become a law, and series of laws, unto himself, surrounding and providing for, not only his own personal control, but his relations to all other individuals and to the State; and that while other theories, as in the past histories of nations, have proved wise enough, and indispensable perhaps for their conditions, *this*, as matters now stand in our civilised world is the only scheme worth working from, as warranting results like Nature's laws, reliable, when once established, to carry on of themselves.

So much, nowadays, we would all claim to see and admit; but, it is to be feared, for the most part with a kind of lip-service and formal adhesion. It was Whitman's greatness that he explored and promulgated all the tremendous assumptions and obligations involved in that comforting creed. During the eighty years that have followed the writing of *Democratic Vistas*, in spite of the fact that we have endured two wars, even more atrocious than the Civil War which served to open yet wider Whitman's wide-open eyes, and that these wars were fought, not only ostensibly but really, to maintain Democracy, we seem to have got no further in the way of understanding and conceiving and imagining Democracy, than to suppose it is achieved and realized in the establishment of adult suffrage for men and women. That is concrete, we seem to say, and comprehensible; that is the universal yardstick, by applying which we know whether or not Democracy exists. But beyond that, everything is vague and shadowy, uncertain and insecure. Do we recognize as essential to Democracy the divine right of a minority to freedom of thought and expression and association? We hardly know. Do we declare, as essential to Democracy, that this right must be denied to a minority which seeks to undermine and overthrow and abolish even that divine right of a minority in which we vaguely believe? We hardly know. The truth is that once the obvious, elementary and mechanical condition of Democracy has been satisfied in universal suffrage, perplexity involves the urgent question: what are the further fundamental moral postulates of Democracy, even on the overtly political plane? It is as though the wind of inspiration had dropped, and the proud ship drifted becalmed. She has not even steerage way.

Granted that some of the problems with which Democracy is now confronted belong to a dimension of which Whitman had no inkling, it remains true that he alone faithfully and passionately explored the hidden moral and religious bases of Democracy from which alone an answer to all its new problems can hopefully be sought. And the main substance of his discovery is that Democracy can be secured only on the foundation of its own appropriate and necessary religion. The notion of a new religion tends, perhaps justly, to be suspect. But Whitman meant no more, but no less, than that, just as Democracy can only be understood as a growth out of former organizations of society, yet must be recognized as something entirely new, so its necessary religion will incorporate and transmute all that is valid in the religions of the societies which preceded it.

My faith is the greatest of faiths and the least of faiths,
Enclosing worship ancient and modern and all between
    ancient and modern.

Thus, in *Democratic Vistas*, he begins by explicitly declaring that Democracy is the development, in the further field of social organization and material opportunity, of the message of Christ that the nature of the individual soul is so transcendent that it sets all men on a common level. Democracy is the implementation of the equality of souls proclaimed by the founder of Christianity. But what is the soul? Whitman has no doubt at all that a soul distinct from the body is an illusion. Body and soul are one, not two. And whether we like it or not, it seems plain that this is the fundamental religious postulate of Democracy, however unsuspected it may be.

That, says Whitman anyhow, is what we discover when as free individuals we explore the reality of what we are. We find an ultimate and indefeasible unity of ourselves of soul and body: an individual One, which at the moment of its awareness of itself, is known to be part of the universal One. Thus that infinite worth and uniqueness of the individual, on which Democracy purports to be grounded, is a reality only when it is pursued to its religious recesses in an ultimate and immediate self-knowledge of what he calls 'the identified soul'. It is notable how close Whitman quite independently comes at this point to the language and ideas of Keats in his famous letter on 'the world as a Vale of Soul-making'. The following crucial declaration of Whitman's might be incorporated bodily into Keats's letter, without alteration and without perceptible discrepancy.

> Religion, although casually arrested, and, after a fashion preserved in the churches and creeds, does not depend at all on them, but is a part of the identified soul, which, when greatest, knows not bibles in the old way, but in new ways – the identified soul, which can really confront Religion when it extricates itself entirely from the churches, and not before.

So close is the resemblance between Whitman's and Keats's thought here that Keats supplies a better gloss than does Whitman himself on his key-phrase, 'the identified soul'. For this is exactly what Keats meant when he distinguished a Soul from an Intelligence. 'There may be intelligences or sparks of the divinity in millions – but they are not Souls till they acquire identities, till each one is personally itself.'

This religious-ethical realization, says Whitman, is the true basis of Democracy; for it is at this point, and at this point only, that the individual becomes a reality. Short of this point, he is an illusion, on which nothing solid or durable can be built. Hence the transcendent importance for enduring Democracy of the emergence of prophets of true 'personalism', as he calls it. This promulgation of 'the religious element which is, finally, at the core of Democracy' is the work of the poet-prophet, the distinctive *literatus* of Democracy. He will work, just as the poet-prophets of former ages and former modes of society, by creating a compulsive image of the concrete, unified personality which is now required, with all its particular and essentially new emotional aptitudes and ethical and religious axioms. Of such poet-prophets of Democracy Whitman claims to be a forerunner, but no more. He is, as it were, the warning and encouraging voice of the interregnum, while Democracy is still unaware of the need of imaginative patterns adequate to its own unconscious assumptions and potentialities – and dangers. The dangers he sees clearly – most apprehensively in 'the long series of tendencies, shapings, which few are strong enough to resist, and which now seem, with steam-engine speed, to be everywhere turning out the generations of humanity like uniform iron castings.'

All of which, as compared with the feudal ages, we can yet do nothing better than accept, make the best of, and even welcome, upon the whole for their oceanic practical grandeur, and their restless wholesale kneading of the masses – I say of all this tremendous and dominant play of solely materialistic bearings upon current life in the United States, with the results as already seen, accumulating, and reaching far into the future, that they must either be confronted and met by at least an equally subtle and tremendous force-infusion for purposes of spiritualization, for the pure conscience, for genuine esthetics, and for absolute and primal manliness or womanliness – or else our modern civilization, with all its improvements, is in vain, and we are on the road to a destiny, a status, equivalent in its real world, to that of the fabled damned.

§

The process of spiritualization which alone can save Democracy from moral disaster Whitman here defines as consisting in three things. First, the awakening of the pure conscience, which is, of course, not pure in the puritan sense, because it includes a candid and delighted recognition of all the mysteries of sex – a recognition inseparable from the knowledge of our participation in and dependence upon the infinite. This knowledge is the immediate source of the pure conscience, because it binds us, with a new sense of obligation, both to the One and to our fellow-men. It is the discovery of a new and deeper meaning in the Christian summons that we shall become, by knowing ourselves to be, 'sons of God'. Second, the establishment of absolute and primal womanliness and manliness: the condition in which 'the men believe in the women and the women in the men'. By which he means the creation of a bond of true love between them, whereby they entirely trust each other: which involves, above all, for Whitman, as for Blake before him, the abolition of sexual secrecy. Man and woman recognize, revere, and delight in each other as palpable manifestations of the divine. They acknowledge their several and mutual dependence upon the infinite, each with his own sense of responsibility. Thirdly, there is genuine aesthetics – the establishment of an ideal and image of attainable beauty, moral and physical, in the common consciousness, which will attract the aspirations of men and women, and serve them as a criterion to judge themselves and others: an image and ideal corresponding to the καλὸς κἀγαθὸς of the Greeks, the *vir pietate gravis* of the Romans, the *honnête homme* of seventeenth-century France, or the Christian gentleman of English-speaking peoples. But these were ideals evolved in and appropriate to aristocratic societies, and almost exclusively masculine. The new ideal image must be consubstantial with the new society, in which men and women are equals and lovers, and men and men comrades; it must arise from and be prophetic of Democracy 'which alone', Whitman says magnificently, 'on anything like Nature's scale, breaks up the limitless fallows of humankind and plants the seeds of personalism'.

In this sense Whitman conceived himself as a poet-prophet co-operating with the silent workings of Democracy, and making communication to the responsive among its members of an image of the new democratic man. Yet image-making, though it was his chosen phrase, and indeed the best he could use to describe his purpose, is inadequate to what he tried to do, and did. He made a total communication of himself. His work was at once less and more than a poetic achievement. There is splendid and immortal poetry in it: perfectly formed and crystalline gems in the mass of ore. But they, without the matrix which surrounds them, would lose the greater part of their significance. And, indeed, we need them less for what they are in themselves, than as the immediate and indisputable evidence that in Whitman was a truly great poet, judged by the most conservative standards. But the matrix is more important than the gems; the total Whitman far more dynamic, far more charged with potential for humanity, than his perfected utterances. The Whitman who gropes his way from the basis of his deep and new-discovered personality, his 'identified soul', into the vast variety of his incomplete affirmations; who offers himself with all his hesitations, his contradictions, and his deep unformulable faith, to his comrades of the future, is a truly prophetic man. He is, in part, the attractive image of the citizen of the new completely human society of which the crude integument is what we call Democracy; he is, in a yet more important part, the tongue-tied soul in travail of the idea of which he is the instinctive vehicle. And this part of him, which is quite inseparable from the other, is perhaps even more durable than the image of the rounded man which he communicates. For it is inherent in this conception of Democracy, as the constant, endless breaking of the fallows of humankind for the sowing of the seed of personality, that it should never reach finality. The process is as recurrent and illimitable as the labours of the veritable husbandry of the earth. Seed-time and harvest, the quiescence of winter frost, and saving and selection of new seed, the ploughing and the fight against the weeds –

> These shall go onward the same
> Though dynasties pass.

So with the process of Democracy. Its faith will never be finally uttered; the final utterances will always be of faiths not its own. The image of its citizen will never be completed. Always there will be the need, to urge it onward, of that sacred and consecrated band of brothers of which Whitman dreamed.

Yet I have dreamed, merged in that hidden-tangled problem of our fate, whose long unravelling stretches mysteriously through time – dreamed out, portrayed, hinted already – a little or a larger band – a band of brave and true, unprecedented yet – armed and equipped at every point – the members separated, it may be, by different dates and States, or south, or north, or east, or west – Pacific, Atlantic, Southern, Canadian – a year, a century here, and other centuries there – but always one, compact in soul, conscience-conserving, God-inculcating, inspired achievers, not only in literature, the greatest art, but achievers in all art – a new, undying order, dynasty, from age to age transmitted – a band, a class, at least as fit to cope with current years, our dangers, needs, as those who, for their times, so long, so well, in armour or in cowl, upheld and made illustrious, that far-back feudal, priestly world. To offset chivalry, indeed, those vanished countless knights, old altars, abbeys, priests, ages and strings of ages, a knightlier and more sacred cause today demands, and shall supply, in a New World, to larger, grander work, more than the counterpart and tally of them.

Whitman the incomplete, sustained by the inward knowledge that his own sincerely acknowledged and avowed incompleteness would make him for ever contemporary with the pioneers of responsible personality on whom the vitality, and even the continued bare existence, of the new and experimental society of Democracy will ultimately depend, is he who deserves our deepest homage. This is the man who retains, and will increase his power to stir the thoughts of men in their dumb cradles. The compulsiveness of his certainty that the person is real only in the measure of his felt and known obligation to higher powers with which he can have immediate contact; his abiding sense of the transparent miracle of personal identity – 'miracle of miracles, beyond statement, most spiritual and vaguest of earth's dreams, yet hardest basic fact, and only entrance to all facts'; his refusal to push the mystery away from the field of immediate experience, by interposing the apparatus of conventional theologies; his brave and humble confidence that 'the last best dependence is to be on humanity itself, and its own normal full-grown qualities, without any superstitious support whatsoever'; his serene assurance that only this gradual, tentative, exploring attitude applied to the whole – not an arbitrary part – of a man's experience is adequately and fully religious, and that 'faith, very old, now scared away by science, must be restored, brought back, by the same power that caused her departure – restored with new sway, deeper, wider, higher than ever' – these are some of the crystallizations from the marvellous and harmonious flux of creative intuitions which Whitman has conveyed to us with all the richness of their matrix of experience. 'My opinions,' he said gently to Traubel, 'are all, always, so hazy . . . though, to be sure, when they come, they come firm.' Both statements are true; but one is often neglected. Whitman's opinions are firmer and more durable than is easily believed.

The Plays of T. S. Eliot

The Plays of T. S. Eliot

*

MR. T. S. ELIOT is a very difficult poet. Many books have already been written to elucidate his poems. I have read two of them; and (as perhaps I might have expected) I found them quite as difficult as the poems they elucidated, and much less exciting. I have neither the desire nor the ability to add to this corpus of commentary. But since it appears to me that there are at least two kinds of difficulty in Mr. Eliot's poems: the difficulty of the texture – the close-wrought and allusive diction, and the difficulty of the under-lying body of thought, I have entertained the idea that in his plays, which are necessarily simpler in diction than his poems, it may be possible to distinguish and isolate at least one important element in his thought which, once recognized, may throw some illumination – if only a sidelight – on some obscure, and sometimes very beautiful, passages of his poetry.

Speaking roughly, we may say that in Mr. Eliot's poetry since *The Waste Land* there has been manifest a twofold movement. While his poetry has become more recondite, his poetic drama has steadily tended to approach more nearly to the level of ordinary experience and communication. The poetic diction has steadily come nearer to ordinary speech. Even of *The Cocktail Party* Mr. Eliot himself has said:

I laid down for myself the ascetic rule to avoid poetry which could not stand the test of strict dramatic utility: with such success, indeed, that it is an open question whether there is any poetry in the play at all.

In *The Confidential Clerk* the process has gone still further. The verse reaches a degree of assimilation to ordinary speech such that it is impossible in the theatre for the ordinary ear to discern, without the book, that the play is not in prose. And parallel with this there has been a progressive elimination of what may be called the supernatural element in his plays. The Tempters, in *Murder in the Cathedral*, the Eumenides in *Family Reunion*, dwindle to the Guardians in *The Cocktail Party*; and the element finally disappears altogether in *The Confidential Clerk*.

The movement towards naturalism is very marked, and evidently deliberate. What it signifies we can only guess; and guessing is unprofitable. But one consequence of it is that the willing suspension of disbelief is not so freely given. The moral and religious issues with which Mr. Eliot is concerned in his plays emerge from the poetic and symbolic penumbra; they become actual and liable to judgment.

§

The earliest of Mr. Eliot's plays, *Murder in the Cathedral* is the remotest from this liability to judgment. The moral and religious issue belongs to a historical past so distant that it is impossible to assimilate it to any predicament of our own. Thomas à Becket goes, open-eyed, to his death and his martyrdom in obedience to what he believes to be the will of God.

He refuses to lift the sentence of excommunication he has pronounced against the bishops who, in obedience to the King, have repudiated his authority: to be absolved, they must go to Rome. He himself is the servant of the Pope, and through the Pope the servant of God. That he did well, we may believe; for we are persuaded, after he has listened to the Tempters and repelled them, that he was sincerely convinced that he was doing as God required – at that time. But one wonders, perhaps as a matter of mere speculation, what Mr. Eliot would have made of the martyrdom of Edmund Campion, or of Archbishop Laud, or perhaps more pertinently still of King Charles the Martyr; or what his real reply would be to Hugh de Morville's exculpation:

At another time, you would condemn an Archbishop by vote of Parliament and execute him formally as a traitor, and no one would have to bear the burden of being called murderer. And at a later time still, even such temperate measures as these would become unnecessary. But, if you have now arrived at a just subordination of the pretensions of the Church to the welfare of the State, remember that it is we who took the first step. We have been instrumental in bringing about the state of affairs that you approve. We have served your interests; we merit your applause; and if there is any guilt whatever in the matter, you must share it with us.

We do not, indeed, permit de Morville to get away with it. Becket's, we say, was a murder, and not an execution. But was Laud's? And was King Charles's? And were they too both martyrs?

We ask the questions only to indicate how remote from the human condition, as we experience it today, is the issue of *Murder in the Cathedral*: a good deal more remote, for example, than the issue in Shakespeare's *Richard II*. And if it be said that the issue between obedience to God and obedience to the State is as urgent today as ever it was, it must be replied that the issue has now assumed a totally different form – even in those countries beyond the iron curtain where there is a bitter struggle between the Communist state and the Roman Catholic Church.

§

It is when Mr. Eliot begins to treat of contemporary characters in his plays that actuality and perplexity also begin. The first of these is *Family Reunion*. The drama plays in an ancient house called Wishwood. There, a generation before the action begins, a loveless and unhappy relation – 'there was no ecstasy' – between a gentle-minded aristocrat and a subtly domineering wife was interrupted by an episode of impassioned love between the husband and his wife's sister, Agatha, who understands his misery. In consequence the man was visited by an impulse to kill his wife, who was carrying their first child. But Agatha restrained him for the sake of the child who 'should have been hers', and in some spiritual sense was hers. She then severed all connection with her lover and the family; and the father, after two more children had been lovelessly born to him, left his home and died in exile. Harry, his first-born, brought up in complete ignorance of this previous history, under the chill shadow of his self-willed and self-righteous mother, marries a woman who resents his mother's domination. She drags him away from Wishwood, and for seven years they spend an unhappy wandering life together. On an ocean voyage he is tempted to push her overboard. Whether he actually does so, is never made clear. But she is drowned, and he feels that he is guilty of her murder. The sense of guilt pursues him. Thus pursued he is returning home when the play opens: to resume his position as the head of the house, determined for him by his mother, at a family reunion on her birthday. For this occasion, Agatha, drawn by her sense of Harry's need, has returned to Wishwood for the first time since her love-affair with his father.

The dramatic action consists in Harry's liberation from his sense of guilt and defilement – from his imprisonment in a private, curse-haunted and intolerable universe. This liberation is gradual and progressive. The first stage is one of utter despair, when Harry, looking through the window on to the assembled family party, realizes that the release he hoped for is not there. There, for the first time, he *sees* his pursuers as objective presences, the Eumenides. But this proves to be a sign of coming salvation. The next stage is in his conversation with his cousin Mary, who was brought up with him at Wishwood. She speaks to him of their common childhood memories, mainly of constraint and unhappiness, and he begins to feel dimly that the secret of his misery lies there, and that there is a possibility of liberation. The third stage is in his conversation with Warburton, the doctor, whom he questions about his father.

I want to know more about my father.
I hardly remember him, and I know very well
That I was kept apart from him, till he went away.

Warburton is evasive and merely tells that his father and mother separated; but Harry, exploring his own memories, now recalls that the death of his father was the crucial moment.

> I remember the silence, and the hushed excitement
> And the low conversation of triumphant aunts.
> It is the conversations not overheard.
> Not intended to be heard, with the sidewise looks,
> That bring death into the heart of a child.
> *That* was the day he died. Of course.
> I mean, I suppose, the day on which the news arrived. . . .
>
> Yes, I see now. That night, when she kissed me,
> I felt the trap close.

Inadvertently Dr. Warburton has revealed that for fuller knowledge he must go to Agatha. Harry's conversation with her is the last stage of his liberation. She tells him of the love between her and his father, and of his father's naïve plans to kill his mother, while she was carrying Harry. Agatha had prevented them, for love of the unborn child.

With that knowledge, Harry's release begins. He can look without fear on the Eumenides.

> Here I have been finding
> A misery long forgotten, and a new torture,
> The shadow of something behind our meagre childhood,
> Some origin of wretchedness. Is that what they would show
>   me?

And he has a sudden experience of happiness.

> I feel quite happy, as if happiness
> Did not consist in getting what one wanted . . .
> But in a different vision.

A decision comes to him and Agatha together. He must leave Wishwood for ever. That means the demolition of the careful, self-willed structure of his mother's plans. Since Dr. Warburton has warned him that any shock will be fatal to his mother, by sticking to his resolution Harry consents to her death. At his departure she dies. Harry moves forward into a life in a different dimension.

> I have not yet had the precise directions.
> Where does one go from a world of insanity?
> Somewhere on the other side of despair.
> To the worship in the desert, the thirst and deprivation,
> A stony sanctuary and a primitive altar,
> The heat of the sun and the icy vigil,
> A care over lives of humble people,
> The lesson of ignorance, of incurable diseases.
> Such things are possible. It is love and terror
> Of what waits and wants me, and will not let me fall.

Most of this makes a convincing and impressive pattern, with manifest affinities to part of the Oresteia. Amy is presented as a modern and respectable Clytemnestra. The origin of wretchedness appears to lie in her lack of love for Harry's father. That, in a sense, kills the father, and shuts the prison on his son, who is deprived of his father's love and is made merely the instrument of his mother's steely determination to keep the family in being. Harry, by escaping at the same moment from his spiritual isolation, and from the bondage of his mother's will, kills her. But these affinities to the Oresteia are formal rather than essential; they seem to have helped the poet in the structure and apparatus of his drama, and in particular to have suggested the use of the Eumenides. But the gulf between the religious conception of the Greek tragedian and that of Mr. Eliot is vast. There are suggested overtones, too, which are totally alien to the Greek mind: above all, perhaps, the intimation that the love in Agatha's soul is the means of salvation from the consequences of lovelessness. It partly released the father; it wholly releases the son. From this aspect, Agatha's profound saying:

> Love compels cruelty
> To those who do not understand love

appears to be the key of the play.

But one element in the play seems to be recalcitrant to this patterning. It is the happening on which all the initial emphasis falls. Harry has at least consented to the death of his wife. Did he push her overboard? Did he only imagine that he pushed her? That is left perplexingly vague. Equally important is an answer to the question: Is there a real and causal connection between Harry's father's desire to kill Amy, and Harry's impulse to kill his wife? By some scale of values – remote indeed from those of the everyday world – but nevertheless acceptable, Harry's father's impulse to murder Amy is condonable, as a naïve and desperate manifestation of the cruelty which love compels towards those who do not understand it. But Harry's impulse to murder his wife has apparently no such justification. Are we then to regard it as an ungovernable impulse caused by a hereditary taint or curse? And how does Harry, in 'the different vision' of the moment of his release, regard it?

Agatha seems to sweep these problems aside in her momentous conversation with Harry.

Harry: Perhaps my life has only been a dream
Dreamt through me by the minds of others. Perhaps
I only dreamt I pushed her.

Agatha: So I had supposed. What of it?
What we have written is not a story of detection
Of crime and punishment, but of sin and expiation.
It is possible that you have not known what sin
You shall expiate, or whose, or why. It is certain
That the knowledge of it must precede the expiation.
It is possible that sin may strain and struggle
In its dark instinctive birth, to come to consciousness
And so find expurgation. It is possible
You are the consciousness of your unhappy family,
Its bird sent flying through the purgatorial flame.
Indeed it is possible. You may learn hereafter,
Moving alone through the flames of ice, chosen
To resolve the enchantment under which we suffer.

We must pause over this. We can allow that, in an ultimate
moral judgment, Agatha's 'What of it?' is admissible: that so
far as the soul of Harry is concerned it is indifferent whether
he killed his wife or dreamed of killing her, if he desired to kill
her. But is it indifferent whether he desired to kill her of his
own volition, or under the mysterious compulsion of a 'curse'?
Is there a condition attainable by the human spirit for which
this distinction is unimportant and unreal? And is it a valid
condition, to be sought after? Or not rather one which is as
remote from the truth as the antipodal condition – that
described by Harry as 'the awful privacy of the insane mind' –
in which *every* human action is felt to be defiled?

Amid several thoughts that are possible, Agatha declares that one is certain: that Harry must know what sin and whose he is to expiate, before he can expiate it. And presumably Harry comes to that knowledge. But we do not: the nature of the sin is withheld from us. Harry's question: 'Where does one go from a world of insanity?' is perhaps deliberately ambiguous. (Is it a private, or an objective world?) But the powerful, though vague, suggestion is that all human life which is not consciously directed to the expiation of an indefinable and omnipresent and all-defiling sin is insanity. And it does not appear that the dramatist has really made up his mind whether Harry's condition was extraordinary, or typical of the human condition. It is surely very important that he, and we, should know. And it is difficult to admit the validity of a possible defence, namely, that although the particular events were extraordinary, they are, nevertheless, symbolic of the universal human condition. That begs the question, which is whether an inherited 'curse' of this extraordinary nature, can be symbolical of the human condition, or convincingly made to appear so.

The problem may be put in another way. What is it that Harry sees in his moment of 'different vision'? Is it a chain of necessity which leads from Amy's lack of love to Agatha's love and his father's desire to murder Amy, thence to his own imprisonment in a loveless and insane private world; and, more mysteriously still, to either the delusion that he murdered his own wife or the actual murder of her, and yet onward to the beginning of his liberation by Agatha's love? And – a pattern within the pattern – does he see that Agatha's and his father's love, equivocal and imperfect, has had two kinds of consequences, two collateral lines of descent: one, from its element of impurity, through desire to murder an offending wife, to the delusion of murder, or murder itself, of an unoffending one; the other, from its element of purity, through Agatha's own solitary suffering, to a power of liberating Harry from the extreme and phantasmal suffering he had endured. That vision would give a satisfying meaning alike to Harry's cry:

> That is the way things happen.
> Everything is true in a different sense,
> A sense that would have seemed meaningless before.
> Everything tends towards reconciliation
> As the stone falls, as the tree falls. And in the end
> That is the completion which at the beginning
> Would have seemed the ruin.

and to Agatha's mysterious incantation:

> A curse comes to being
> As a child is formed. . . .
> A curse is like a child, formed
> To grow to maturity:
> Accident is design
> And design is accident
> In a cloud of unknowing.
> O my child, my curse,
> You shall be fulfilled.

That is all deeply imagined: yet an obstinate and invincible doubt remains. Can Harry really understand *why* his father's impulse to murder his wife had revisited him in circumstances so different, and in so much more appalling a form. And if he does understand the necessity of this, to what power did he ascribe the necessity? To the Greek Fate or to the Christian God?

While studying *Family Reunion* in and for itself, one is inclined to suspect that the fundamental cause of this persistent perplexity lay in the very nature of the poet's effort to reinterpret a theme of Greek tragedy in terms of a modern consciousness. The Chorus declares:

> And whether in Argos or in England
> There are certain inflexible laws
> Unalterable, in the nature of music.

It may be so; but we cannot help demanding to glimpse them. In *Family Reunion* they elude our vision. We cannot accept that the chain of guilt and retribution which began with the sacrifice of Iphigenia and ended with the absolution of Orestes is manifested anew in the chain of guilt which connects Harry's impulse to murder with his father's: for precisely this latter connection is doubtful. Is it real? Ought it be real for any mind that has undergone the absolution of Christianity? Does a sin endure to be expiated by the next generation?

§

Almost as though Mr. Eliot sympathized with, if not shared, this perplexity, his next play, *The Cocktail Party*, takes up again the theme of expiation from sin, and frees it from the entanglements of the suggestion of a hereditary curse. The subjects of salvation, Edward Chamberlayne, Lavinia his wife, and Celia his mistress, do not suffer for the sins of their fathers. The cause of the misery from which they are liberated is not in the distant past, like Harry Monchensey's, neither do they labour, like him, under any dreadful delusion. In consequence, there is no need of oracular utterance in the play: there are no mysteries to conceal or reveal. This is no doubt the chief reason why *The Cocktail Party*, as compared with *Family Reunion*, achieved a great and deserved success with the public. On the surface it is, from first to last, eminently credible. Even the paradox by which the at first sight futile, but distinctly comic, Julia and Alex are subsequently revealed as confederates with Riley-Reilly in the work of salvation strains our credulity only enough to make us meditate its significance. At the same time, when we come to essentials, the relation between the two plays is seen to be close indeed.

The affinity between Celia's process of salvation and Harry's is evident, and the relation between her previous state of mind and his obvious. If we abate what is extraordinary in Harry's condition and consider it as one which might, without straining, be universalized, we have more or less exactly Celia's condition, when she realized that the love between herself and Edward is illusory.

Celia: No . . . it isn't that I *want* to be alone,
        But that everyone's alone – or so it seems to me.
        They make noises, and think they are talking to each
            other;
        They make faces, and think they understand each other.
        And I'm sure that they don't. Is that a delusion?

Reilly: A delusion is something we must return from.
        There are other states of mind, which we take to be
            delusion,
        But which we have to accept and go on from.

Celia's condition is awareness of isolation, and a sense of sin –
not for anything she has done:

> But of emptiness, of failure
> Towards someone, or something, outside of myself;
> And I feel I must . . . *atone* – is that the word?

That is, in essence, Harry's condition at his moment of en-
lightenment. But Celia has also an affinity with Agatha. She
has had a love-affair with Edward, which she does not repent,
and which she describes in retrospect very much as Agatha
describes her love for Harry's father. Celia says:

> I haven't hurt *her*.
> I wasn't taking anything away from her –
> Anything she wanted.

Which is almost identical with Agatha's words to Amy:
'What did I take? Nothing that you ever had.' And Celia's
description of her experience of love:

> I have thought at moments that the ecstasy is real
> Although those who experience it may have no reality.
> For what happened is remembered like a dream
> In which one is exalted by intensity of loving
> In the spirit, a vibration of delight
> Without desire, for desire is fulfilled
> In the delight of loving . . .

recalls Agatha's: 'There are hours when there seems to be no
past or future. . . .' The affinity between Celia and Agatha is

perhaps not to be stressed, but it is sufficiently marked to warrant the suggestion that Celia is, in some sort, a combination of Harry and Agatha: a combination which is natural enough, for the spiritual relation between Harry and Agatha is intimate indeed.

But in *The Cocktail Party* the guidance which in *The Family Reunion* arises as it were spontaneously between Agatha and Harry, or rather comes to them:

> Oh, mother
> This is not to do with Agatha, any more than with the rest
>   of you,
> My advice has come from quite a different quarter. –

is objectified in Reilly's advice to Celia. This makes for more explicit dramatic action; it is also necessary in so far as Agatha and Harry are combined in Celia. The dialogue between Harry and Agatha would have to be soliloquy in Celia, were it not for the creation of Reilly. And Reilly has something more to say than is said, or hinted at, in the dialogue between Harry and Agatha. There is now a second possibility other than the life of expiation and dedication. Reilly says to Celia:

> If that is what you wish,
> I can reconcile you to the human condition,
> The condition to which some who have gone as far
>   as you
> Have succeeded in returning. They may remember
> The vision they have had, but they cease to regret it,
> Maintain themselves by the common routine,
> Learn to avoid excessive expectation,

Become tolerant of themselves and others,
Giving and taking, in the usual actions
What there is to give and take. They do not repine;
Are contented with the morning that separates
And with the evening that brings together
For casual talk before the fire
Two people who know they do not understand each
other,
Breeding children whom they do not understand
And who will never understand them.

Celia: Is that the best life?

Reilly: It is a good life. Though you will not know how good
Till you come to the end. But you will want nothing
else,
And the other life will be only like a book
You have read once, and lost. In a world of lunacy,
Violence, stupidity, greed . . . it is a good life.

But Celia clings to her vision, and rejects, not without
regret, the good life that Reilly offers.

I feel it would be a kind of surrender –
No, not a surrender – more like a betrayal.
You see, I think I really had a vision of something
Though I don't know what it is. I don't want to forget it . . .
I couldn't give anyone the kind of love –
I wish I could – which belongs to that life.

So Celia chooses the second way, which Reilly describes to
her.

The second is unknown, and so requires faith –
The kind of faith that issues from despair.
The destination cannot be described;
You will know very little until you get there;
You will journey blind. But the way leads towards possession
Of what you have sought for in the wrong place.

That pilgrimage is indistinguishable from Harry's; and Celia's actual destiny is a factual and painful fulfilment of Harry's conjecture.

> Somewhere on the other side of despair.
> To the worship in the desert, the thirst and deprivation,
> A stony sanctuary and a primitive altar, . . .
> A care over lives of humble people,
> The lesson of ignorance, of incurable diseases.
> Such things are possible.

The difference, if difference there is, between Celia and Harry – abating the Orestean pattern, which is irrelevant when we are considering the poet's doctine of salvation – lies in the fact that the vision to which Celia clings is a vision vouchsafed to her in the illumination of love. But here again, although it is not certain that Harry's vision was of this kind, there is some evidence to suggest that it was. For it is central to the drama of *Family Reunion*, as I read it, that liberation comes to Harry through Agatha's love and his recognition of it, both as a fact in the past and an illumination in the present. That is the purport of his cry to Agatha:

> And what did not happen is as true as what did happen
> O my dear, and you walked through the little door
> And I ran to meet you in the rose-garden.

The rose-garden is the symbol of the same ecstasy of love which Celia describes, when

> what happened is remembered like a dream
> In which one is exalted by intensity of loving
> In the spirit, a vibration of delight
> Without desire, for desire is fulfilled
> In the delight of loving.

Agatha, with Harry's father, 'only looked through the little door When the sun was shining on the rose-garden'. But when she has told her secret to Harry she 'walks through the little door' and he 'runs to meet her in the rose-garden'. It is not pressing the poet's symbolism too hard to interpret passing through the little door as the attainment of love beyond desire, and looking through it as the vision of such love when it comes to one entangled in desire. Agatha's love for Harry and Harry's response to it are an instantaneous and eternal passing through the little door.

One would surmise, too, that Harry's 'running to meet Agatha in the rose-garden' is the experience he describes at the moment of its happening in the words:

> Look, I do not know why,
> I feel happy for a moment, as if I had come home.
> It is quite irrational, but now
> I feel quite happy, as if happiness
> Did not consist in getting what one wanted
> Or in getting rid of what can't be got rid of
> But in a different vision. This is like an end.

Or, if the experiences are not identical, they are complementary. There is, therefore, some solid ground for supposing that

Celia's experience is, at the spiritual level, indistinguishable from Harry's.

What is new, in the scheme of salvation in *The Cocktail Party* as compared to *Family Reunion* is the destiny allotted to Edward and Lavinia. They, who have been so estranged that Edward has sought consolation in Celia, and Lavinia in Peter, now accept each other and their life together. They are presented at the end of the play as having

Become tolerant of themselves and others,
Giving and taking, in the usual actions
What there is to give and take. They do not repine . . .
Two people who know they do not understand each other,
Breeding children whom they do not understand
And who will never understand them.

It is the path Celia has refused when Reilly offered it, on the ground that it would be a kind of betrayal of the vision or the experience she had when she was in love with Edward. 'I couldn't give anyone the kind of love which belongs to that life.' But, in spite of the fact that Reilly, in answer to her question: 'Which way is better?' assures her:

Neither way is better.
Both ways are necessary. It is also necessary
To make a choice between them –

we do not believe him. Indeed, he himself says the way of – shall we call it? – tolerant acceptance in marriage, involves a surrender of the vision of love.

And the other life will be only like a book
You have read once, and lost.

In spite of Reilly's assurance, therefore, that neither way is better than the other, the way of man-woman love is, in fact, presented as inferior.

This very important issue is rather clouded by the particularities of the two situations: of Edward's and Lavinia's relation, and Edward's and Celia's. There is no suggestion that Edward and Lavinia ever did love one another. As surely as between Amy and Harry's father in *Family Reunion*, between Edward and Lavinia 'there was no ecstasy'. And between Edward and Celia, the ecstasy was wholly on Celia's side. When the test came, she discovered that there was no 'new person, *us*';

> And then I found we were only strangers
> And that there had been neither giving nor taking
> But that we had merely made use of each other
> Each for his purpose. That's horrible.

Horrible, indeed; the discovery is humanly true and not infrequent. But surely it cannot be universalized as the inevitable and inexorable destiny of lovers. That Celia is tempted to universalize it is natural enough in her moment of disillusion.

> Can we only love
> Something created by our own imagination?
> Are we all in fact unloving and unlovable?

But Reilly himself appears to accept this. The best that can happen to a man and woman who have experienced the illusion of loving each other, of being a new person in their union, is the tolerant mutual acceptance of 'two people who know they do not understand each other'.

> They may remember
> The vision they have had, but they cease to regret it.

Lose it, they must; the only questions are whether they remember it at all, and whether, if they do, they learn the wisdom to cease to regret it. The ecstasy of love is, in so far as it is attached to persons, an illusion. Says Celia:

> I have thought at moments that the ecstasy is real
> Although those who experience it may have no reality...
>   But what, or whom I loved,
> Or what in me was loving, I do not know.

If there is love, there are no persons; if there are persons there is no love. The new person, the Thou-and-I of true lovers, is an illusion. Such appears to be the doctrine. It is surely untrue to the experience of many. However often it may happen that the ecstasy of romantic love does not survive marriage, there remain many cases in which the enchantment only deepens with the years: married couples who, in spite or because of the ordinary trials of existence, have learned to love each other far more fully than they did when they fell in love. This precious possibility of common experience is simply denied by Mr. Eliot in *The Cocktail Party*. The utmost he allows is that a man and a woman who experience the ecstasy of love should make in marriage the best of a bad job, by realizing that they do not, and cannot, understand one another, and that they are, by nature, unloving and unlovable. It may seem profound; but it is false to human experience. This mutual tolerance is not the best that can happen to a man and a woman who do not choose the way of renunciation. On the contrary: they can learn to love one another, and therefore to understand one another, fully as persons, and become truly lovable in the process, which contains its own discipline of self-renunciation. But this is definitely excluded from the scheme of salvation of *The Cocktail Party*.

That does not prevent it from being an admirable play. It is. Given the particular human situation, the resolution of it is convincing enough. It certainly makes a good thing out of that particular human predicament. The new recognition (as compared to *Family Reunion*) that there are two ways of salvation is not only spiritually true, but it makes possible a dramatic contrast which is finally convincing as well as immediately effective. Compared with it, the contrast in *Family Reunion* between Harry and Agatha and Mary on the one side, and Harry's aunts and uncles and brothers on the other, seems artificial and strained; so that we seem to be offered a truly desperate choice between complete renunciation and complete idiocy. But in *The Cocktail Party*, the double contrast between Celia on the one hand and Edward and Lavinia on the other, and between Edward and Lavinia in their former and in their latter condition is at once illuminating and satisfying. The doubt that insinuates itself arises not from what happens to these particular characters but from the doctrine proclaimed in the play.

§

There is no such felt inevitability about the happenings in Mr. Eliot's latest play, *The Confidential Clerk*. The situation there presented to us is extraordinary in the extreme. A prosperous financier, Sir Claude Mulhammer, married rather *de convenance* to the eccentric daughter of an earl, has had, before his marriage, an illegitimate son (Colby) and daughter (Lucasta) by two different mothers; or at least so he believes. The mother of Colby he had passionately loved, but she had died in childbirth. Lady Elizabeth, his wife, it is revealed in the course of the play, also has had a son before marriage, with whom she has completely lost contact. Sir Claude has kept affectionately but remotely in touch with his. The action of the play begins when Lady Elizabeth is returning from a long holiday abroad. During her absence Sir Claude has brought in Colby to replace his retiring confidential clerk (Eggerson), and he is now planning with Eggerson how best to induce his wife to take to Colby and wish to adopt him, in the hope that he may then be able to tell her outright that he is his son. When the plan of campaign is settled, Sir Claude departs and Colby enters. Shortly afterwards, Lucasta attended by her fiancé, B. Kaghan, bursts in; and Colby is distinctly overwhelmed by such an apparently hard-boiled young lady. Sir Claude re-enters, just as Eggerson is off to meet Lady Elizabeth at the airport; but before he has time to be gone, her ladyship arrives under her own steam. Satisfied and indeed exalted by her contact with Colby's aura, she instantly adopts him and takes over the decoration of the flat which is being prepared for him. Eggerson and she then depart; and Colby, a little unnerved by such a baptism of fire, is left alone with his father. It emerges in their conversation that Colby is a disappointed organist and is having a struggle to overcome his old ambition in his new job; that Sir Claude is also a disappointed artist; and that both have the yearning to escape, through the practice of art, 'from a sordid world to a pure one'. For both it 'takes the place of religion'. Sir Claude has, however, accepted the heritage of his father's business, by way of atonement for his own rebellious misunderstanding of his father when he was a boy. Colby explains that is not possible for him.

> You have always been his son
> And he is still your father. I only wish
> That I had something to atone for!
> There's something lacking, between you and me,
> That you had, and have, and always will have, with your
> father . . .
> The father who was missing in the years of childhood.
> Those years have gone for ever. The empty years.

There roughly the first act ends: it is distinctly dull, for it has been occupied with the exposition of a fantastically com- plicated situation. The audience is more or less prepared, by her behaviour, for the knowledge that Lucasta is Sir Claude's daughter, though Colby is not; more or less prepared too for Colby and Lucasta to fall in love with each other: which in the second act they proceed to do. Colby is playing his new piano to her in his new flat – the first time he has played to anyone 'since I came to the conclusion that I should never be a musician'. We know what that means: he is trying to take her into his world. And she, it is apparent, wants to be taken there. The scene between them is admirably done. Gradually Lucasta throws off her mask, as Colby confesses his desire to have someone with him in his 'secret garden', which is never quite real to him because he is always alone there.

Lucasta: Can no one else enter?

Colby: It can't be done by issuing invitations:
They would just have to come. And I should not see
them coming.

I should not hear the opening of the gate.
They would simply . . . be there suddenly,
Unexpectedly. Walking down an alley
I should become aware of someone walking with me.
That's the only way I can think of putting it.

Lucasta: How afraid one is of . . . being hurt!

They draw nearer and nearer to each other, till finally Lucasta tells Colby she is Claude's daughter. Colby naturally is struck dumb. The gate of his garden is closed, and she is outside it. Since he dares not tell her that he is Sir Claude's son, she completely misunderstands the nature of his evident shock, and believes he despises her as a bastard. Just at the moment when Colby decides to break his promise and tell her the truth, her breezy fiancé enters. Lucasta goes off with him under the influence of her devastating misapprehension. At that moment Lady Elizabeth enters, and when she learns from Colby that he is an illegitimate child and has been brought up by a Mrs. Guzzard, comes to the conclusion that he is *her* son, and tells her husband so. The act ends with both of them claiming Colby.

In the third act Mrs. Guzzard is summoned to settle the problem. While they are awaiting her Lucasta enters to apologize to Colby, who is not in the room, and to announce that she is really going to marry Kaghan. 'But for Colby', she says bitterly, 'I would never have come to appreciate B.' Sir Claude then tells her that Colby is his son and her brother (though Lady Elizabeth of course demurs), and she understands the real nature of Colby's shock at her own disclosure. After her departure Mrs. Guzzard arrives and it is gradually revealed, first, that Mrs. Guzzard did take charge of Lady Elizabeth's child; but the child is not Colby, but Kaghan: and second, that Colby is not Sir Claude's son, but Mrs. Guzzard's own perfectly legitimate one – the son of Herbert Guzzard, a disappointed organist. Colby then decides to leave Sir Claude, and become an organist too.

> As long as I believed that you were my father
> I was content to have had the same ambitions
> And in the same way to accept their failure.
> You had your father before you, as a model;
> You know your inheritance. Now I know mine.

Sir Claude is heartbroken. And the play ends with the suggestion that Colby will become a priest.

What are we to make of all this? The complications are so intricate and artificial that one is bewildered and tempted to ask whether *The Confidential Clerk* has a meaning at all, in the sense that *Family Reunion* and *The Cocktail Party* had? There are moments when I could almost believe that Mr. Eliot is playing a practical joke on that very considerable public which holds, as it were *de fide*, that he must be saying something very profound – all the profounder because they do not understand it.

§

Any attempt to interpret *The Confidential Clerk* from an ordinarily human standpoint must begin with the situation between Colby and Lucasta in Act II. At that point the play is emotionally real to an ordinary person. Two human beings deprived of any warm human relation during their childhood, move towards one another: and their movement is delicately presented. The pathos of the situation lies in Colby's not having time to explain to Lucasta the nature and cause of his shock at her disclosure that she is also Claude's child. But Colby, having summoned up his courage to tell her the truth, is prevented only by the entry of Kaghan at the critical moment. There is nothing inevitable about that; it is merely good theatre. So that we have a right to expect that Lucasta's pitiful misunderstanding will be resolved: she will know that she and Colby are at least united as the victims of a common tragedy. They will be able to love one another: differently indeed, but it will still be love. But at this moment, with the entry of Lady Elizabeth, comes the glimmer of a better possibility. Colby may not be Claude's son after all. This in view of our concern over him and Lucasta, means for us that there is a possibility that they may emerge from their loneliness into a natural love.

In Act III, however, it is slowly revealed that Colby is not Lady Elizabeth's son, as she imagines. But that is of importance only as maintaining the dramatic tension. For a moment, Colby *is* Claude's son: therefore Colby's and Lucasta's love is hopeless. But then, it is finally and decisively revealed that he is not Claude's son. Therefore Colby and Lucasta are free to come together. That is the conclusion which our emotional concern over them is bound to draw.

But this expectation is quite deliberately frustrated by the dramatist. Lucasta has meanwhile given up Colby and turned to Kaghan. Why? Apparently, simply because of her disastrous misunderstanding of Colby's shock. Colby, she thinks, despises her and she comes to appreciate Kaghan who does not. So her decision to marry Kaghan depends entirely upon the mere accident of Kaghan's interruption. She, indeed, gives other explanations. She asserts that 'B. needs me'; but that does not satisfy, because we do not know how or when she has discovered this. And nothing in what has passed between Colby and herself in Act II justifies her in saying, *after* she has learned the true reason for his shock:

> Colby doesn't need me
> He doesn't need anyone. He's fascinating
> But he's undependable. He has his own world,
> And he might vanish into it at any moment –
> And just at the moment when you needed him most!
> And he doesn't depend upon other people, either.

If that is true of Colby, it is not for any reasons made manifest in the play – quite the contrary. He had replied directly to Lucasta's

> You don't seem to me
> To need anybody.

Colby: That's quite untrue.

And Lucasta has accepted it, as any ordinary reader or spectator does. That indeed makes the pathos of the scene between them.

Why then does Lucasta suddenly revert to her old mistaken judgment of Colby at the very moment when the true cause of his shock at her disclosure is revealed – at the very moment, that is, when she knew how desperately he had needed her? Why does she persist in saying to him 'You don't care enough'? Has she really become insensitive and devoid of imagination? Why? How?

If, on the other hand, we are to believe that Colby was quite mistaken in rejecting the imputation that 'he needed nobody', and that Lucasta really understood the truth about him all along, one can only repeat that nothing in Act II has prepared us for such a valuation of him.

Hence, Act III produces in us a deep bewilderment, which becomes extreme when Lucasta is apparently quite unimplicated and unconcerned when it is finally revealed that Colby is not Claude's son at all.

Because of this central bewilderment, the revelations in this last act produce upon us, both in performance and in reading, the effect of mere complications. Why should Kaghan be Lady Elizabeth's son? It has the status of an odd and improbable fact without significance. And even the revelation that Colby is the son of Mr. and Mrs. Guzzard – the son of a disappointed organist – will hardly carry the significance which seems to be attached to it. We are told that this knowledge satisfies Colby, that it makes his way plain to him, that he must follow his father, as an organist, in order that he may know him. But that information brings no real conviction. And even if, by an intellectual effort, we try to relate it to the adumbrations of the spiritual bond which exists between father and son, as propounded by Claude in Act I, we cannot make the connection emotionally real. We seem to be moving in a hazy world of psychological abstractions – of mere intellectual possibilities.

So that Colby himself ends by bewildering us. We try to put him together. We say to ourselves that, while he believed that Claude was his father, and above all when he learned that Claude was a disappointed artist like himself who had become content to follow his father's line and thus to know him, he too was content to follow the same pattern; but that the something in Colby which still 'rebels against accepting the conditions which life has imposed' is premonitory of the revelation that

Claude is not his father. But this pattern is complicated by Colby's sense of a vacuum –

> The father who was missing in the years of childhood.
> Those years have gone for ever. The empty years.

The real bond of father to son is missing. That sense of void we understand, or think we do. And the effect of it, surely, would be to make Colby hungry for a relation of love: which leads naturally, or with dramatic inevitability, to the pathos of the situation with Lucasta in Act II, of which a true resolution is denied, we feel, by a mere theatrical expedient which, because it is not superseded by a real resolution, ends by making Lucasta incredible.

That line of understanding Colby being thus cut off, one reverts, *faute de mieux*, to accepting that Colby finds his relation of love with the figure of his organist father. But one cannot accept this heartily, because the revelation that Claude is not Colby's father has removed the obstacle between him and Lucasta. And the artificiality of the means by which they have been separated now becomes positively oppressive. Why should Colby so tamely acquiesce in it? If there have been, as Lucasta says, profound changes in them both since their encounter in Act II – 'We've changed since then' – those changes have not been made apprehensible to us. And we cannot fairly be asked to take them on trust. Colby's statement towards the end of Act II, when his parentage has become wholly doubtful: 'I don't feel tonight that I ever want to marry' seems merely transient: to indicate nothing more than that at the moment his chief desire is to have his doubts resolved. If it is intended to betoken a substantial change in his attitude to Lucasta, it will not carry the weight.

At the end of Act III Colby, by reason of some further obscure inward change, now would like a father dead, obscure and silent.

> An ordinary man
> Whose life I could in some way perpetuate
> By being the person he would have liked to be
> And by doing the things he had wanted to do.

This wish is immediately granted. He discovers that his father was an obscure organist who – we have previously learned from a remark of Mrs. Guzzard – had strong views on the necessity of infant baptism, and was presumably a convinced and practising Christian. Colby immediately decides to follow him, and the final suggestion is that he will go one better and take orders. So he will find the love he needs. But this is a development in Colby for which we have not been prepared. From his attitude in Act II –

> If I were religious, God would walk in my garden
> And that would make the world outside it real
> And acceptable, I think –

even if we took his words at face value, to his final position, is an enormous stride. And why and how he takes it is quite unexplained, unless we are to interpret his allegiance to an unknown mortal father as symbolic of a discovery of God: which is an excessive strain on our poetic faith. And anyhow, we are not permitted to take Colby's words at face value: the particular emotional context in which they are set is that of his and Lucasta's mutual attraction, and there they inevitably take on the meaning: 'If I were religious, God would walk in my garden and absolve my loneliness; but I am not religious, so let it be you, Lucasta, who enter and walk with me.'

Thus we are returned again to the question: *Why* do Lucasta and Colby renounce each other? The order in time is that Lucasta renounces Colby first. And this seems to be quite without real cause. (Her misunderstanding of Colby's shock cannot persist as a *real* cause, because it is completely removed in Act III.) And Colby appears to renounce her equally without real cause.

Yet the playwright has created a situation such that we demand a valid cause why these two, apparently in need and in reach of each other, should be separated. Yet he offers us none: and we feel frustrated and baffled. We have never been made to feel and *believe* that Lucasta believes that Colby needs nobody; or that it is true of Colby. We have never been made to feel and *believe* – indeed, it is not hinted – that Colby finds, in the mere fact that Lucasta should have thought him shocked in the way she did, a gulf between them.

In simple human terms, he has turned Lucasta into a monster. How can she say almost at the same moment that she now understands Colby's behaviour, when she learns she is his sister, and that he was 'much too . . . detached ever to be shocked in the way I thought you were'? Those two statements are quite irreconcilable. And he has turned Colby into something incomprehensible. Is his 'I don't care enough?' and his 'That's me, is it?' – genuinely baffled, or bitterly ironical? We do not know; and we are given no clue. The playwright has aroused our emotional sympathies only to lead them into a wilderness. And we feel we have been cheated.

The Plays of T. S. Eliot

§

The family likeness of *The Confidential Clerk* to *The Cocktail Party* and *Family Reunion* is fairly plain. Colby, with his eventual vocation for the priesthood, is a successor to Harry and Celia; Lucasta and Kagan correspond to Edward and Lavinia. And the underlying doctrine of love between a man and a woman is the same. The conspicuous difference in this respect is that in *The Confidential Clerk* for the first and only time Mr. Eliot depicts the birth of love (and very well he does it) whereas formerly he presented it only as faded ecstasy, or a memory of an illusion *à deux*. In consequence he has to spend a good deal of effort on destroying the possibility of love that he has created. But he notably fails to make this withering of a nascent love inherently convincing. It almost shocks by its artificiality. It appears not to arise from anything in the characters themselves, nor from insuperable circumstance, but to be quite arbitrary.

Sic volo, sic jubeo; sit pro ratione voluntas.

Indeed it is achieved only at the heavy cost of making his lovers psychologically incredible. In order to make them tread the now familiar alternative paths of ascetic vocation on the one hand and unloving marriage on the other, they are turned into puppets.

Presumably, from his own point of view, Mr. Eliot is merely depicting two innocent young victims of the momentary illusion of romantic love that they 'understand one another', who are providentially saved from disaster by the misunderstanding which occurs between them. But this interpretation is unnatural for an audience which does not share the dramatist's radical scepticism of falling in love, and could only be made plausible to it by explanations which he does not give. In either case – whether the audience is too naïve to appreciate Mr. Eliot's irony, or Mr. Eliot too sceptical to appreciate its natural reactions – his doctrine remains the same. Whatever else may endure, romantic love does not. Sooner or later, it is revealed as illusion. Love ceases to deceive only when it is transferred from a person to God. Such, when Mr. Eliot has descended to a level at which he is, if not completely comprehensible to us, at least subject to our moral judgment, seems to be an essential part of what he has to say to us.

It is important to recognize this; for it is, in itself, a humanly important idiosyncrasy. Moreover, this radical scepticism of human love is unfamiliar in English drama: one might almost say, uncongenial to its genius. Certainly it is conspicuously antipodal to the ethos of Shakespeare's plays.

And there seems to be a close connection between this asceticism of Mr. Eliot's drama and the particular kind of religious mysticism which has come to preponderate in and be characteristic of Mr. Eliot's pure poetry. It is a mysticism which has little use for the familiar things of earth and little sympathy with the struggles, the delights and the achievements of more ordinary folk. How immense is the gulf which separates from common experience, for instance, the opening lines of the first of the *Four Quartets*!

> Time present and time past
> Are both perhaps present in time future,
> And time future contained in time past.
> If all time is eternally present
> All time is unredeemable.
> What might have been is an abstraction

> Remaining a perpetual possibility
> Only in a world of speculation.
> What might have been and what has been
> Point to one end, which is always present.

They induce, in one reader at least, a sort of intellectual vertigo. Conceivably that was the author's intention; and in a less refractory mind, it might induce a sort of metaphysical awareness, perhaps related to, but not identical with a timeless moment of more familiar experience. The poem continues:

> Footfalls echo in the memory
> Down the passage which we did not take
> Towards the door we never opened
> Into the rose-garden. My words echo
> Thus, in your mind.
>   But to what purpose
> Disturbing the dust on a bowl of rose-leaves
> I do not know.
>   Other echoes
> Inhabit the garden. Shall we follow?
> Quick, said the bird, find them, find them
> Round the corner. Through the first gate,
> Into our first world, shall we follow
> The deception of the thrush? Into our first world.
> There they were, dignified, invisible,
> Moving without pressure, over the dead leaves,
> In the autumn heat, through the vibrant air,
> And the bird called, in response to
> The unheard music hidden in the shrubbery,
> And the unseen eyebeam crossed, for the roses
> Had the look of flowers that are looked at.

Those lines, I scarcely know why, seem very beautiful to me.
They seem to describe, to extract the quintessence of a might-
have-been, as it were experienced now. The rose-garden is in
Family Reunion the symbol of communion in love; and I
imagine it carries the same meaning here. Not that I understand the whole of those lines. I do not know whether 'my
words' that echo the footfalls in memory, are the words with
which the poem begins, or the words which describe the
footfalls; and I do not know in whose mind they echo. But
beyond and perhaps through my perplexities something
precious is communicated: which, translated humanly, is at
once a regret for a communion that was not achieved and an
acceptance of the loss.

The poem continues:

> There they were as our guests, accepted and accepting.
> So we moved, and they, in a formal pattern,
> Along the empty alley, into the box circle,
> To look down into the drained pool.
> Dry the pool, dry concrete, brown edged,
> And the pool was filled with water out of sunlight,
> And the lotos rose, quietly, quietly,
> The surface glittered out of heart of light,
> And they were behind us, reflected in the pool.
> Then a cloud passed, and the pool was empty.
> Go, said the bird, for the leaves were full of children,
> Hidden excitedly, containing laughter.
> Go, go, go, said the bird: human kind
> Cannot bear very much reality.
> Time past and time future
> What might have been and what has been
> Point to one end, which is always present.

There ends the first strophe. And again it seems to me very beautiful, and almost intolerably sad. I think I understand it; or enough of it to be responsive. And it is dimly suggested to me that there is some intimate connection between this poignant exploration of *desiderium* and the occlusion of human love which recurs so obstinately in Mr. Eliot's plays.

Occlusion is a mild word for what happens to love in Mr. Eliot's poetry. *The Waste Land* is a poem which shaped and coloured the consciousness of a whole generation of English intellectuals. A note on the mysterious figure of Tiresias informs us that 'what Tiresias sees is, in fact, the substance of the poem'. And what Tiresias sees is the sordid amour of the typist and the 'young man carbuncular'. The episode is brilliantly done, to its masterly ironic conclusion:

> When lovely woman stoops to folly and
> Paces about her room again, alone,
> She smoothes her hair with automatic hand,
> And puts a record on the gramophone –

but, considered as the substance of the poem, it points to an extremity of disgust with physical love in the author which is disquieting. Besides, we do not need the evidence of his note. The theme returns again and again to an extent which seems positively obsessive. *The Waste Land* is a poem of 433 lines. Yet there are no less than six quite distinct expatiations on the sordidness of physical love. There is first the horrible, but again brilliant, monologue concerning Lil and Albert in the public house; then Sweeney and Mrs. Porter; then the vision of Tiresias; then the three separate destinies of the three Thames daughters. And previous to all these are, seventh and eighth, episodes just outside this particular pattern of nausea indeed, but pictures of the mutual incomprehension and nervous exasperation of lovers: the hyacinth girl in *The Burial of the Dead*, and the players in *A Game of Chess*.

'My nerves are bad to-night. Yes, bad. Stay with me.
'Speak to me. Why do you never speak? Speak.
   'What are you thinking of? What thinking? What?
'I never know what you are thinking. Think.'

I think we are in rats' alley
Where the dead men lost their bones.

It is within the truth to say *The Waste Land* is saturated with a scepticism of love, and a nausea of physical sex. There is no means of deciding whether Mr. Eliot regarded his poem as a faithful picture of the human condition, or as the expression of a private but invincible disgust, which he recognized as a mental sickness. One may, however, say that he did recognize the condition it expresses as one of spiritual inanition, of death in life, from which he sought release. For that is the burden of the poem. It is conceivable that the particular disgust of love was no more than the most vehement and concentrated expression of a total disgust of human life; but that does not correspond to the immediate impact of the poem. The emphasis, as the reader experiences it, is on the exposure and anatomization of love – a process which it is difficult not to connect with some powerful lines in the poem *Gerontion*, which closely preceded *The Waste Land*.

I, that was near your heart was removed therefrom
To lose beauty in terror, terror in inquisition.

I have lost my passion: why should I need to keep it
Since what is kept must be adulterated?
I have lost my sight, smell, hearing, taste and touch:
How should I use them for your closer contact?

The catastrophe of love, by the loss of 'beauty in terror, terror in inquisition' seems, at any rate, aptly to describe the temper and attitude of *The Waste Land*.

After *The Waste Land* the obsessive emphasis on the squalor of sex disappears. Mr. Eliot seems to have attained the release he sought from his condition. The achievement, I have always supposed, is commemorated, and the new condition explored and described in *Ash Wednesday*, though much of it is too hard for my understanding. I can grasp no more than the general drift, which is that the poet has died his death, and found the true object of his love.

And the bones sang chirping
With the burden of the grasshopper, saying

Lady of silences
Calm and distressed
Torn and most whole
Rose of memory
Rose of forgetfulness
Exhausted and life-giving
Worried reposeful
The single Rose
Is now the Garden
Where all loves end
Terminate torment

Of love unsatisfied
The greater torment
Of love satisfied
End of the endless
Journey to no end
Conclusion of all that
Is inconclusible
Word of no speech
Grace to the Mother
For the Garden
Where all love ends.

'The single Rose is now the Garden.' The rose-garden is Mr. Eliot's constant symbol of the ecstasy – the illusory ecstasy – of love between man and woman. The garden and the roses of the illusion, of the fading rainbow that seems to arch between and make one two persons in reality without contact or understanding, are now transmuted into the one Rose of mystical adoration – the only object of love, according to its votaries, which does not deceive.

The same, or a kindred, emancipation was achieved by St. Augustine, or vouchsafed to him. It is valid, no doubt, for those who experience it; and they will be those who desire to experience it. There are others, probably a very much larger number, whose desires are, like Miranda's, more humble; whose demand for perfection is less implacable; or, shall we say, whose philosophy or religion of love, whether instinctive or explicit, is utterly different from St. Augustine's or Mr. Eliot's. They hold that love between mortals is not, inevitably, doomed to disillusion and decay; that it is in origin a vision of the eternal in the perishable, that the vision can be kept and deepened; that the relation, instead of degenerating into a resigned acknowledgment of mutual misunderstanding and impenetrability, can grow, by virtue of 'the little kindnesses which are so many deaths in the Divine Image', to its own fulfilment, not in the memory of a faded ecstasy, but in perpetually renewed delight and gratitude for the visible evidence of the bounty and the love of God. For those who hold this faith, admiration of Mr. Eliot's poetic and dramatic achievement will always be tempered by a sense that the superhuman difficulty of so much of his writing is causally connected with his almost inhuman detachment from the most exalted experience that falls to the lot of the common man.